W9-CGW-564

I WONDER WHY ENCYCLOPEDIA

I WONDER WHY ENCYCLOPEDIA

Kingfisher
NEW YORK

KINGFISHER
Larousse Kingfisher Chambers Inc.
95 Madison Avenue
New York, New York 10016

First American edition 1997
10 9 8 7 6 5 4 3 2 1

This edition copyright © Larousse plc 1996
Material in this edition previously
published by Kingfisher in the *I Wonder Why* series.

All rights reserved under International and
Pan-American Copyright Conventions

LIBRARY OF CONGRESS CATALOGING-IN-PUBLICATION DATA
Kingfisher I wonder why encyclopedia.—1st ed.
p. cm.
Includes index.
Summary: Combines solid information with quirky facts in a question and answer format.
1. Children's encyclopedias and dictionaries. 2. Children's questions and answers. [1. Encyclopedias and dictionaries. 2. Questions and answers.] I. Kingfisher Books.
AG5.K53 1997
031—dc21 97-16449 CIP AC

ISBN 0-7534-5095-X
Printed in France

Project editor: Clare Oliver
Contributing editors: Brigid Avison, Jackie Gaff, Claire Llewellyn
Cover design: Smiljka Surla
I Wonder Why series designer: David West Children's Books

Production manager: Susan Wilmot

Contributing authors: Brigid Avison; Andrew Charman; Anita Ganeri; Christopher Maynard; Richard Mead; Clare Oliver; Amanda O'Neill; Josephine Paker; Steve Parker; Philip Steele; Carole Stott; Barbara Taylor; Rod Theodorou; Brenda Walpole; Jenny Wood

Contributing consultants: Andrew Branson; British Museum: Department of Egyptian Antiquities and Department of Graeco-Roman Antiquities; Michael Chinery; Eryl Davies; Dougal Dixon; Ian Graham; David Haycock, Paul Hillyard; Dr. David Hughes; Keith Lye; Dr. Elizabeth McCall Smith; Geoff Puplett; Dr. Peter Rowan; Peter Thoms

CONTENTS

THE UNIVERSE AND PLANET EARTH

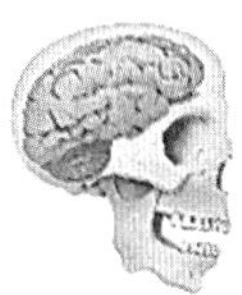

SCIENCE AND THE HUMAN BODY

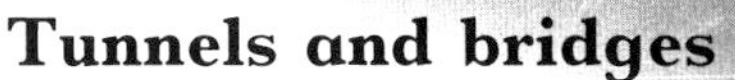

COUNTRIES AND PEOPLES

ANIMALS VOLUME 1

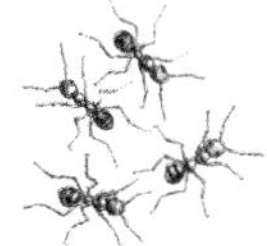

ANIMALS VOLUME 2

THE UNIVERSE AND THE EARTH

What is the universe?

The whole world and everything beyond it is the universe. It is all the stars and planets, the Earth and its plants and animals, you and me — everything.

• You are made of the same stuff as a star!

• There are huge groups of stars in space. They're called galaxies, and they're like gigantic star-cities.

• The Big Bang explosion sent the young universe flying out in all directions. Over vast ages of time, bits came together to make galaxies.

• The galaxies are still speeding apart today, and the universe is getting bigger.

When did it begin?

Many astronomers think that everything in the universe was once packed together in one small lump. Then, about 15 billion years ago, there was a gigantic explosion which they call the Big Bang.

• To see how the universe is getting bigger, watch the dots as you blow up a polka-dot balloon.

Will the universe ever end?

Some astronomers think the universe will just go on getting bigger as the galaxies speed apart. Others think that the galaxies may one day start falling back toward each other until they crash together in a Big Crunch!

• Astronomers are scientists who study the stars and the planets.

• No one knows where all the material to make the universe came from in the first place.

What is the Milky Way?

The Milky Way is the galaxy we live in. It is made up of all the stars you can see in the sky at night, and lots and lots more you can't see.

• The Milky Way is a spiral galaxy. Below you can see what it looks like from above — a bit like a whirlpool with long spiraling arms.

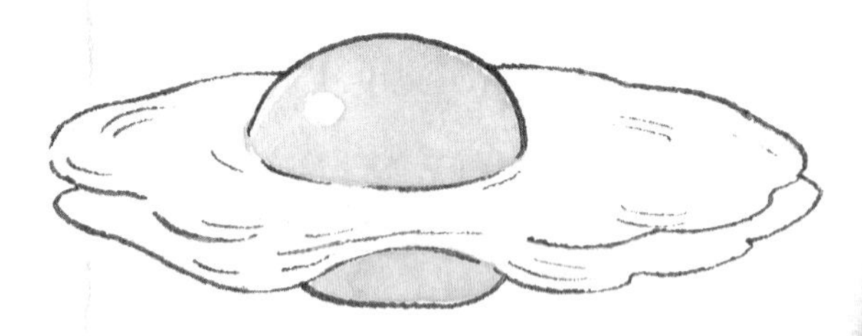

• From the side, a spiral galaxy looks like two fried eggs stuck together.

• The Milky Way got its name because at night we can sometimes see part of it looking like a band of milky white light across the sky.

• We live on a planet called Earth, which travels around a star called the Sun.

• Astronomers usually give galaxies numbers instead of names. Only a few have names that tell us what they look like — the Whirlpool, the Sombrero, and the Black Eye, for example!

• These are the three main galaxy shapes.

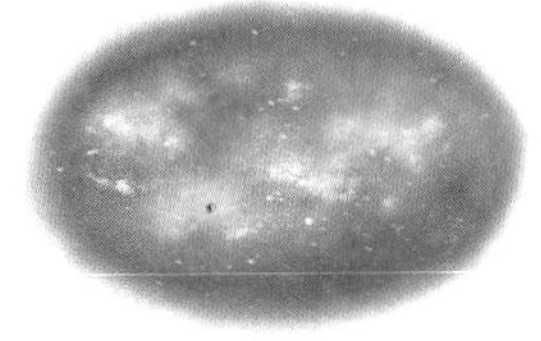

Irregular (no special shape)

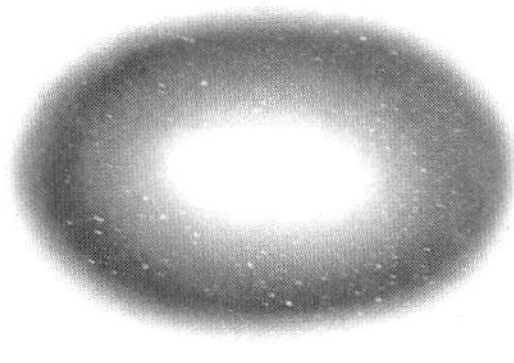

Elliptical (egg-shaped)

Spiral

How many stars are there?

There are about 1,000 billion stars in the Milky Way. That's about 200 stars for every person living on Earth today!

Although we can't see all of it, astronomers have worked out how big the universe is and how many stars it has. There are about 100 million trillion stars, in around 100 billion galaxies. It's hard even to think about so many stars, let alone count them!

What are stars made of?

Stars aren't solid like the ground beneath your feet. Instead, they are made of gases like the air around you.

The two main gases in stars are called hydrogen and helium. They are the stars' fuel. Stars make heat and light from them.

• Sometimes huge flamelike sheets of glowing gas shoot out from a star. These are called prominences.

• Since earliest times, people have seen patterns in the way stars are grouped in the sky. The patterns are called constellations.

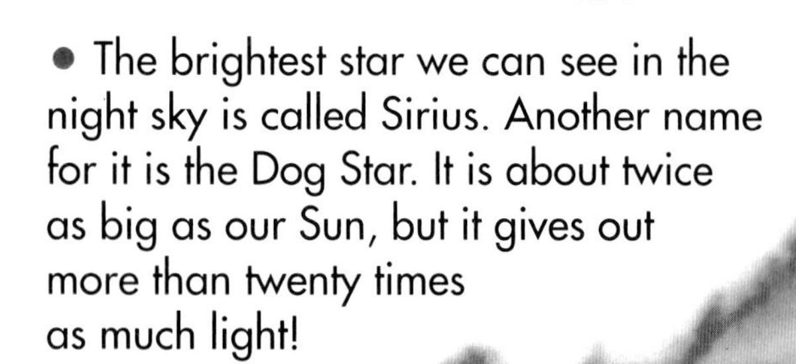

• The brightest star we can see in the night sky is called Sirius. Another name for it is the Dog Star. It is about twice as big as our Sun, but it gives out more than twenty times as much light!

Why do stars twinkle?

Stars only twinkle when we look at them from the Earth. Out in space their light shines steadily. We see them twinkling and shimmering because of the air around the Earth. As light from a star travels toward us, it is bent and wobbled by bubbles of hot and cold air.

• Light bends when it passes through different things. If you put a straw in a glass of water, for example, it looks bent because it is half in air and half in water.

Are stars star-shaped?

No, stars are round, like balls. We give them pointed edges when we draw them because this is what they look like from the Earth, with their light blinking and twinkling.

What is a red giant?

All stars are born, live for a very long time, and then die. A red giant is a huge old star.

• Stars are being born all the time. They start their lives in star-nurseries called clusters.

1 All stars are born in huge spinning clouds of gas and dust. Our Sun was born 4.6 billion years ago.

2 The gas and dust come together to make lots of balls, which become star clusters.

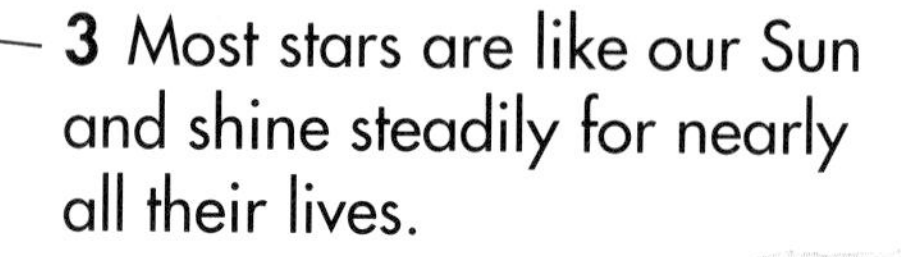

3 Most stars are like our Sun and shine steadily for nearly all their lives.

• If you think of our Sun as shining like a car's headlights, then a red giant would shine like a lighthouse!

4 Toward the end of their lives, stars like our Sun swell up and become as much as 100 times bigger. They turn into red giants. Our Sun will do this in about 5 billion years' time.

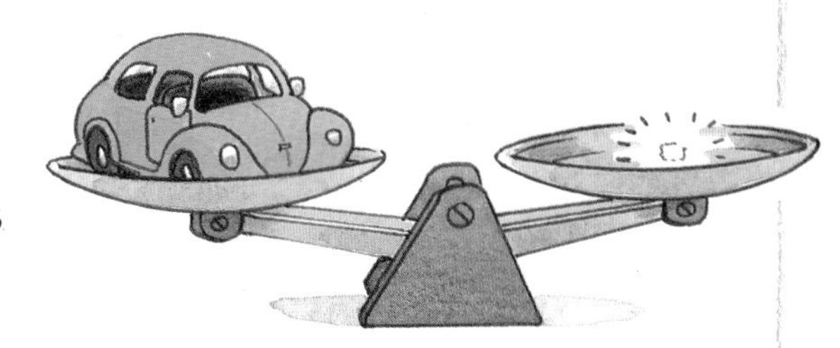

• On Earth, a sugar-lump-sized piece of a white dwarf would weigh as much as a small car!

5 When it has used up all its gas fuel, a red giant shrinks down into a white dwarf. It is then about 10,000 times smaller, but still very hot.

6 The star cools down and ends its life billions of years later, as a black dwarf — a cold black cinder.

Which stars explode?

Different kinds of stars lead different lives. Some stars have a lot more gas fuel in them than others. These really massive stars don't die quietly, by cooling down. Instead, they blow up in a great flash of light. Stars that explode like this are called supernovas.

• Stars must have at least eight times as much gas fuel as our Sun to end their lives in supernova explosions.

How hot is the Sun?

Like all stars, our Sun is a huge ball of superhot gas. It is hottest in the middle — the temperature there is around 27 million °F (15 million °C).

The outside of the Sun is a lot cooler than the middle — only 10,000 °F (6,000 °C). But this is still twenty times hotter than the hottest kitchen oven!

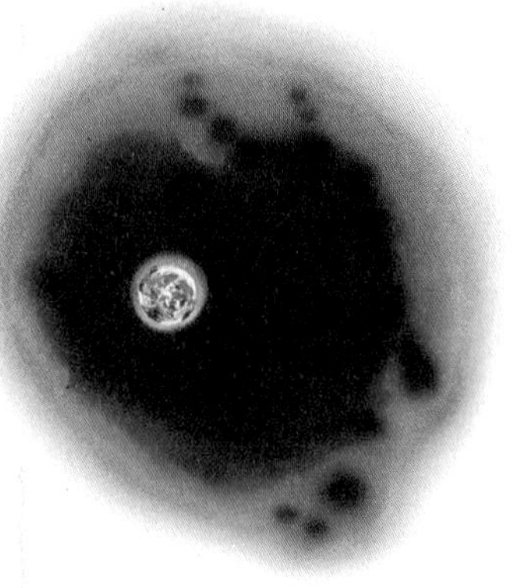

• Dark patches called sunspots come and go on the face of the Sun. They make it look as though it has chickenpox. Sunspots are dark because they are cooler and so give out less light than the rest of the Sun.

• Most sunspots are larger than the Earth.

• Plants and animals couldn't live without the Sun's heat and light.

• The Sun is the only star that's close enough to the Earth for us to feel its heat.The next nearest star to Earth is called Proxima Centauri. Our Sun's light takes 8.3 minutes to reach us, but Proxima Centauri's takes 4.3 years!

• The Sun uses more than 30 million truckloads of fuel every second!

Will the Sun ever go out?

One day the Sun will use up all its gas fuel and die. But this won't happen in your lifetime, or your children's, or even your great-great-great grandchildren's! Astronomers think that the Sun has enough gas fuel to last for at least another 5 billion years.

How many planets are there?

Our planet, the Earth, has eight neighbors. Together they make a family of nine planets which travel around the Sun. We call the Sun, and all the space bodies that whirl around it, the solar system.

Besides the Sun and the planets, the solar system includes moons, mini-planets called asteroids, and comets.

• Comets are a little like huge dirty snowballs. Most stay out on the edge of the solar system, but a few travel close to the Sun. These comets grow gas and dust tails, millions of miles long, when the Sun's heat starts to melt them.

• The word planet comes from the Greek word *planetes*, which means "wanderer."

Mercury

Venus

Earth

Mars

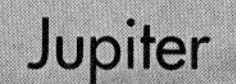

Jupiter

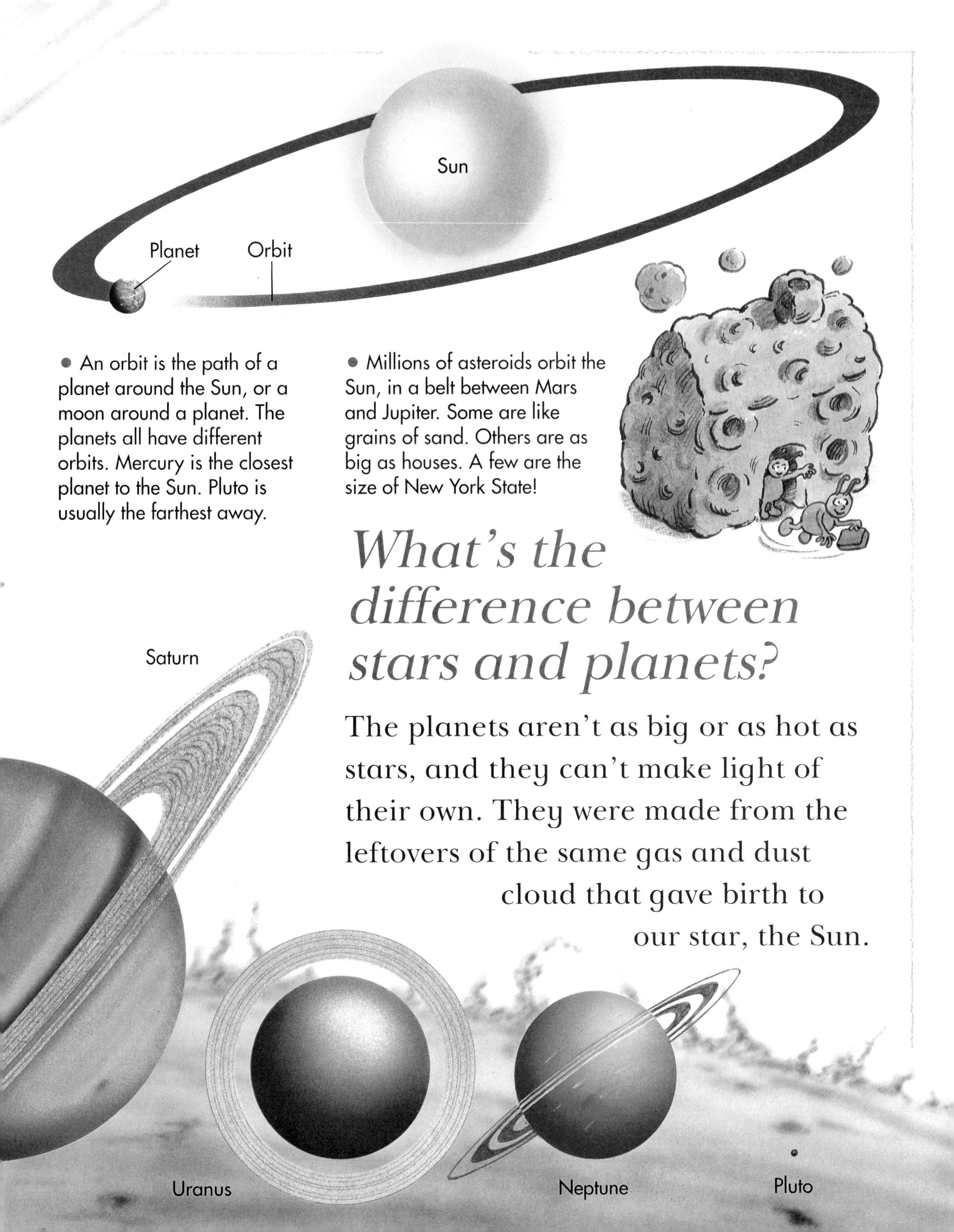

• An orbit is the path of a planet around the Sun, or a moon around a planet. The planets all have different orbits. Mercury is the closest planet to the Sun. Pluto is usually the farthest away.

• Millions of asteroids orbit the Sun, in a belt between Mars and Jupiter. Some are like grains of sand. Others are as big as houses. A few are the size of New York State!

What's the difference between stars and planets?

The planets aren't as big or as hot as stars, and they can't make light of their own. They were made from the leftovers of the same gas and dust cloud that gave birth to our star, the Sun.

Which is the hottest planet?

Venus isn't the closest planet to the Sun, but it is the hottest. The temperature there can reach 900 °F (500 °C) — that's about eight times hotter than it gets in the Sahara Desert, the hottest place on Earth.

• Although Mercury (right) is closer to the Sun, Venus is hotter! This is because Venus is covered by clouds of gas which act like a blanket, keeping in the Sun's heat.

• Space probes have landed on Venus and sent back pictures and information to Earth. The probes were destroyed soon after landing, however, by the terrible climate on Venus.

• Mercury is covered in craters — hollows made by huge space rocks crashing into it.

• If you could visit Mercury, you would see that the Sun looks more than twice as big there as it does from Earth. This is because Mercury is so much closer to the Sun.

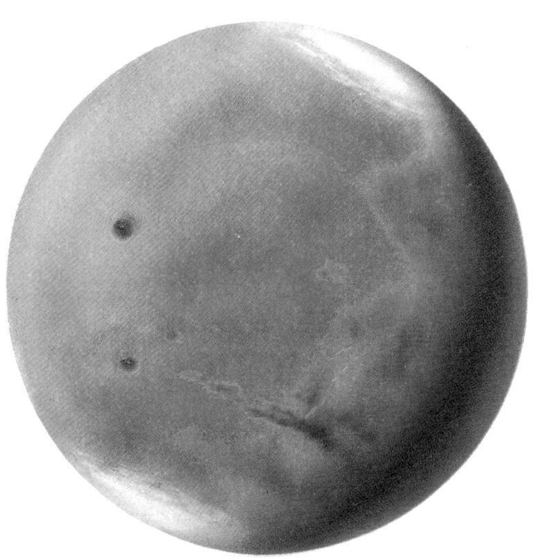

• Living things need water. If there is any on Mars, it is frozen inside its north and south polar ice caps.

• Mars is the next planet after ours from the Sun, and people once thought that like the Earth it might have living things. Space probes were sent, but they didn't find any signs of life!

Which is the Red Planet?

Mars is often called the Red Planet. The ground there is covered in dusty red soil, which gets swept up by the wind to make pink clouds! The rocks on Mars have lots of iron in them, and iron turns red when it rusts. A better name for Mars might be the rusty planet!

Which is the biggest planet?

Jupiter is so huge that all the other planets could fit inside it! The beautiful patterns on its face are made by swirling clouds of gas, stirred up by powerful windstorms.

• Jupiter's Great Red Spot is so big that two Earths could fit inside it! It is a gigantic storm that has been raging for over 300 years.

• Jupiter was named by the ancient Romans, after the king of their gods.

• Jupiter is one of four planets with rings around them.

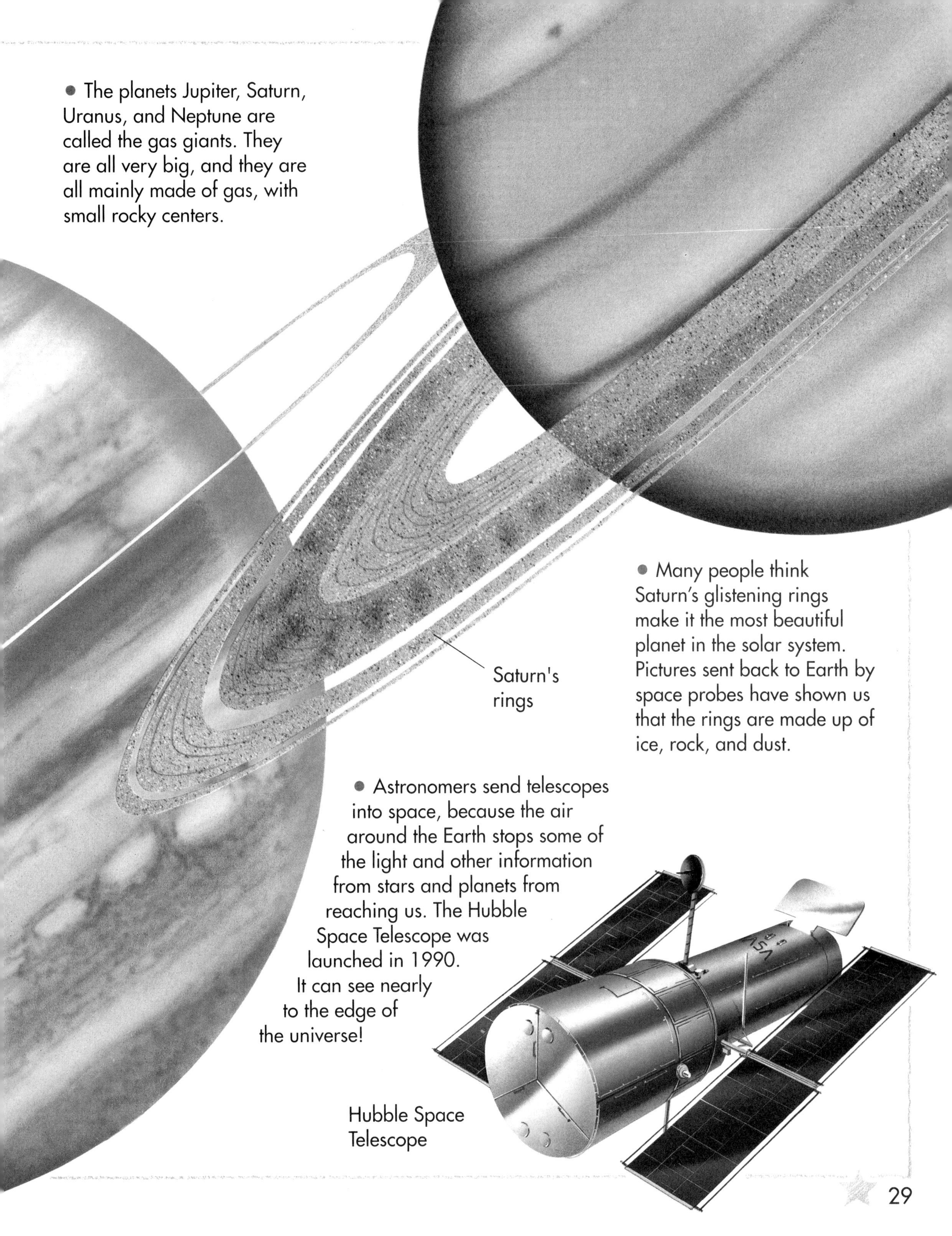

• The planets Jupiter, Saturn, Uranus, and Neptune are called the gas giants. They are all very big, and they are all mainly made of gas, with small rocky centers.

• Many people think Saturn's glistening rings make it the most beautiful planet in the solar system. Pictures sent back to Earth by space probes have shown us that the rings are made up of ice, rock, and dust.

• Astronomers send telescopes into space, because the air around the Earth stops some of the light and other information from stars and planets from reaching us. The Hubble Space Telescope was launched in 1990. It can see nearly to the edge of the universe!

Which planet is farthest from the Sun?

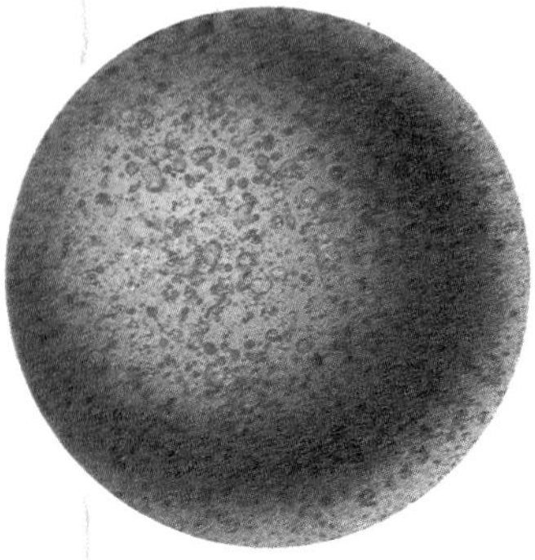

Although for most of the time Pluto is the most distant planet, every 248 years its orbit brings it closer to the Sun than Neptune!

• Between 1979 and 1999, Pluto's orbit makes Neptune the farthest planet from the Sun.

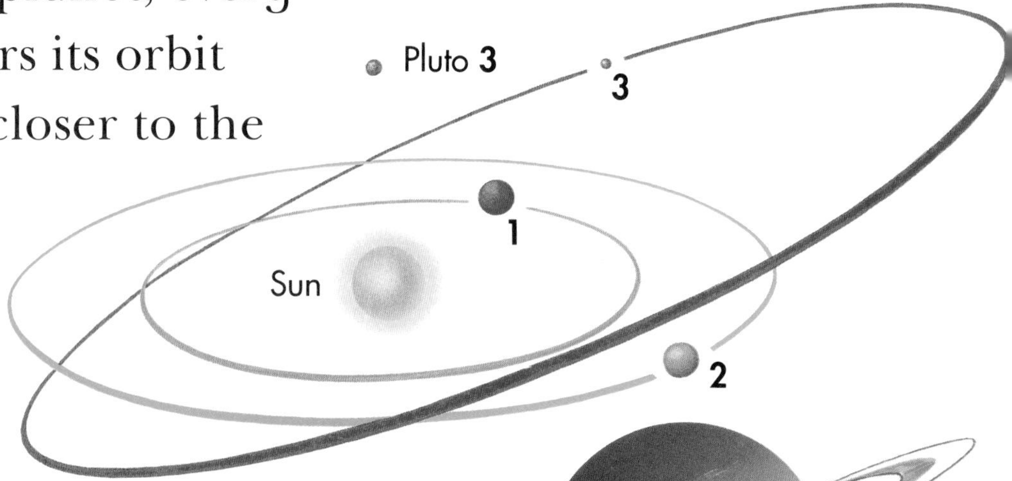

Pluto **3**

Sun

Uranus **1**

Neptune **2**

• One of the gases in Uranus is called methane. It gives the planet its blue-green color.

Which is the coldest planet?

Ice cream would taste as hot as soup on Pluto, where the temperature is an unbelievably icy -400 °F (-240 °C)! Pluto is so cold because it is very far from the Sun. It is almost 40 times farther away than the Earth is.

How do we know about the farthest planets?

Until the U.S. Voyager 2 space probe visited Uranus in 1986 and Neptune in 1989, not a lot was known about these two planets. They are too far away for us to see them clearly from Earth, even through the most powerful telescopes.

Voyager 2's cameras showed that Neptune has eight moons. Earth-based astronomers could only see two using telescopes.

• Voyager 2 left the Earth in 1977 and reached Neptune twelve years later, in 1989.

Is the Earth round?

If you were an astronaut floating around in space, the Earth would look like a gigantic ball. It isn't perfectly round, though. Like a ball that's been gently squashed, it's slightly flatter at the top and bottom, and it bulges out just a little at the middle.

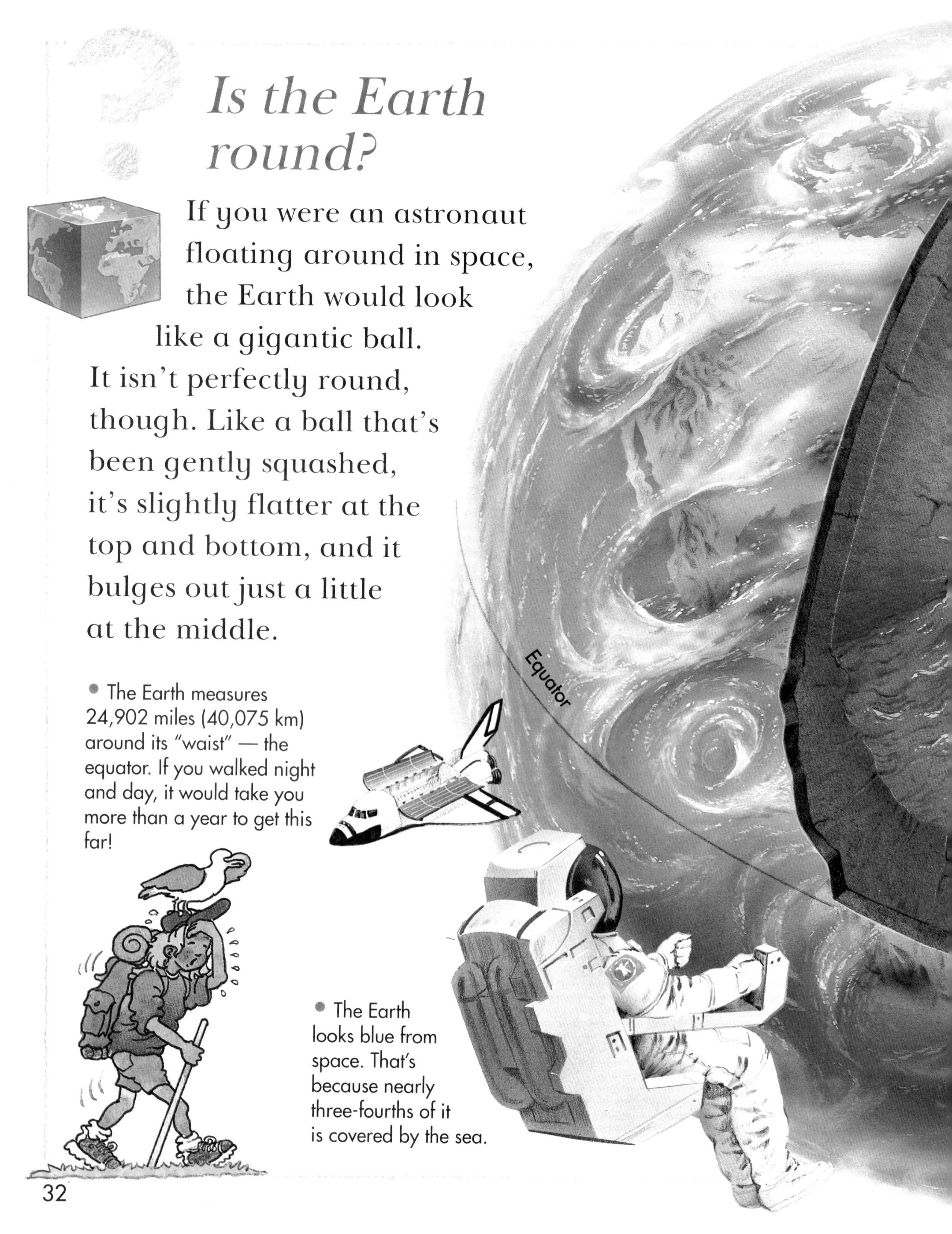

• The Earth measures 24,902 miles (40,075 km) around its "waist" — the equator. If you walked night and day, it would take you more than a year to get this far!

• The Earth looks blue from space. That's because nearly three-fourths of it is covered by the sea.

• It's very hot indeed at the centre of the Earth – more than 5000 °C. That's about 150 times hotter than a really scorching hot summer's day!

What is the Earth made of?

The Earth is made up of different layers of rock and metal. Some of the layers are hard, but others are so hot that they've melted and are runny – a bit like hot sticky toffee.

• The Earth's crust doesn't stop at the seashore. It goes on under the deepest oceans.

How old is the Earth?

Scientists think the Earth formed over 4 billion years ago — although no one was there to see! They think the Moon formed then, too.

• Human beings are very new to the Earth. If you imagine our planet's 4-billion-year-long history squeezed into one year, people have only been around since late on December 31!

▽ About 200 million years ago there was just one supercontinent called Pangaea.

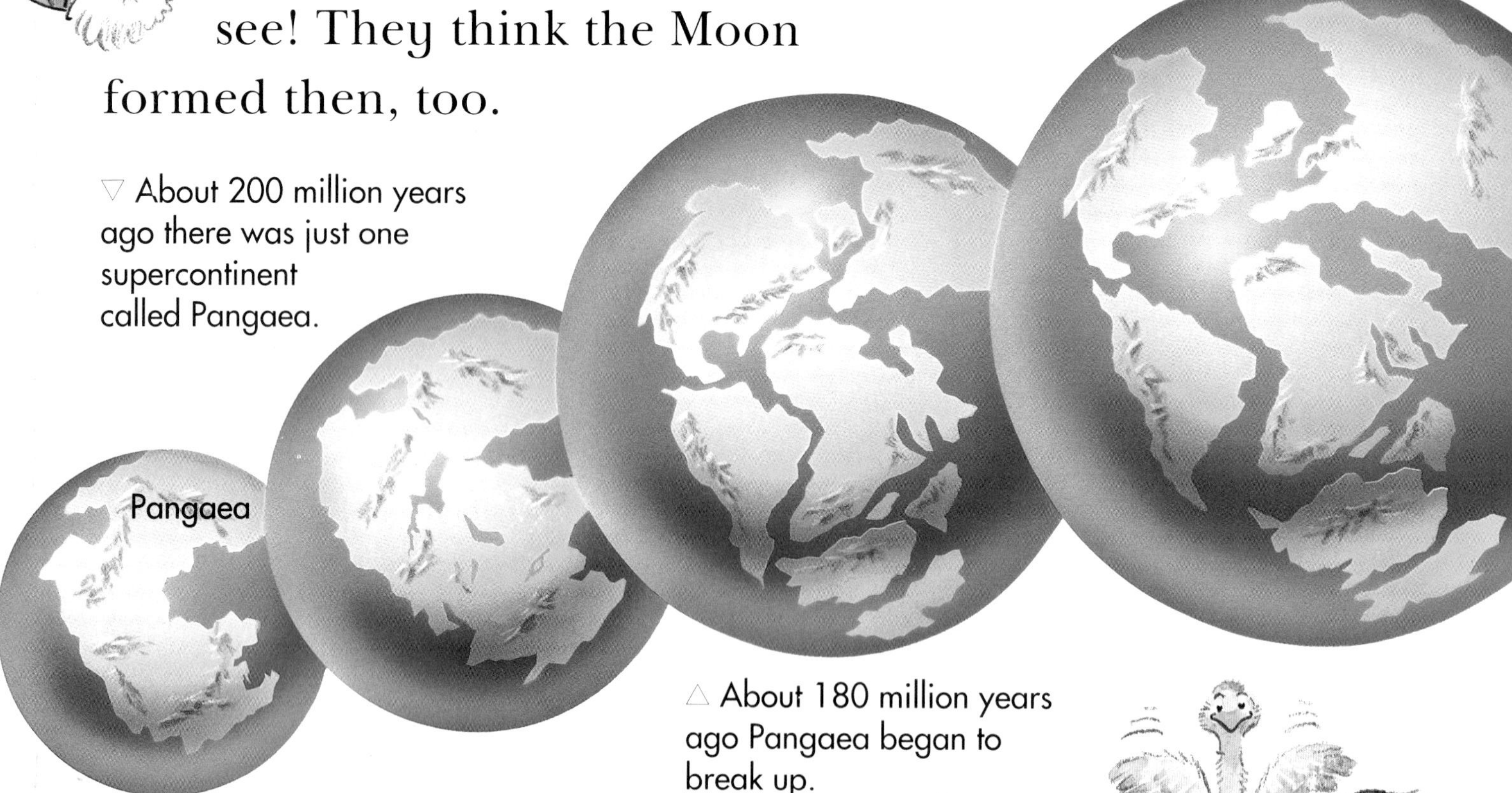

△ About 180 million years ago Pangaea began to break up.

• Continents are massive pieces of land. There are seven of them in all. Trace them from a map, and try to see how they once fitted together.

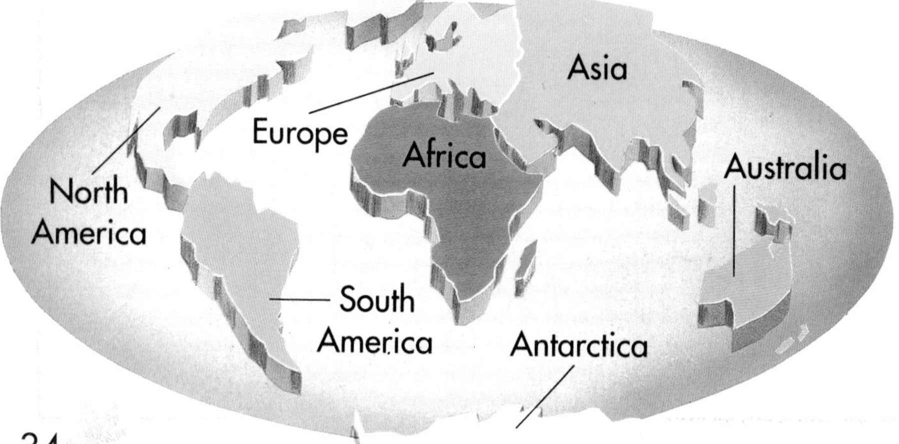

• Emus live in Australia, rheas in South America, and ostriches in Africa. They look similar, and none of them can fly. They may have been related to one kind of bird. It could have walked to all three continents millions of years ago, when the land was joined.

Has the Earth changed much?

Yes, it has! About 300 million years ago, most of the land was joined together in one big piece. Then it began to break up into smaller pieces called continents. These slowly drifted apart, until they reached the places they're in today.

▽ About 65 million years ago the continents drifted farther apart.

▽ Today, the continents are still drifting.

• North America and Europe are still moving apart by about 2 inches (4cm) each year. That's about the length of your thumb.

Where are the highest mountains?

• Himalaya means 'home of the snows'. It's a good name for these freezing peaks.

The Himalayas in Asia are the world's highest mountains. They're so high that they're known as 'the roof of the world'. The towering mountain peaks are bitterly cold places, where the snow and ice never melt.

• These are the highest mountains in each continent:

Asia – Mt Everest 8848 m
S. America – Aconcagua 6959 m
N. America – Mt McKinley 6194 m
Africa – Mt Kilimanjaro 5895 m
Europe – Mt Elbrus 5633 m
Antarctica – Vinson Massif 5139 m
Australia – Mt Kosciusko 2230 m

Can mountains shrink?

Many mountains are getting smaller all the time. Every day, small chips of rock are carried away by ice, snow and running water.

Some mountains are getting bigger, though. The Himalayas are still being pushed up by movements inside the Earth.

• In Hawaii there is a mountain called Mauna Kea which is more than 1,300 metres higher than Mount Everest. Most of it is under the sea, though.

• The higher you go up a mountain, the colder it becomes. Many of the animals that live high up on mountains have thick woolly coats to keep out the cold – goats, llamas and yaks, for example.

Which mountains breathe fire?

Volcanoes are mountains that sometimes spurt out burning ash, gas, and hot runny rock called lava. The gas and fiery lava come from deep down inside the Earth, and burst up through cracks in the crust.

• The saucerlike top of a volcano is called a crater. Sometimes a dead volcano's crater fills with rainwater and makes a beautiful lake.

• There are about 500 active volcanoes on land. There are even more under the sea.

Do people live on volcanoes?

It's a risky thing to do, but many people live on volcanoes — especially farmers. The ash from a volcano makes the soil very rich, so the farmers can grow large crops. They need to be able to run fast though!

• There are volcanoes in space, too. Olympus Mons on the planet Mars is three times higher than Earth's Mount Everest.

• Pilots beware! The ash and dust from a volcano can get inside a plane's engines and stop them dead.

What makes the Earth shake?

The Earth's surface is made up of huge pieces of hard rock which drift on the hot runny rock below. Sometimes these pieces push and shove against each other, making the Earth shake. This is what happens during an earthquake.

• In the worst earthquakes the ground cracks open, streets sink, and buildings crumble to piles of rubble.

• The greatest danger in an earthquake is a building collapsing on top of you. Sheltering under a table or a doorway may save your life.

Can people tell if an earthquake is coming?

Scientists who study earthquakes are called seismologists. Although they know where earthquakes are likely to happen, they usually can't say exactly when.

- People have tried to design earthquake-proof buildings. Some of the latest ones are shaped like pyramids or cones.

- Animals seem to feel the land moving long before we do. Dogs howl, snakes wriggle out of their holes, and chickens run for their lives!

- The people of Ancient China believed that the Earth was balanced on the shoulders of a giant ox. Earthquakes happened when the ox shifted the Earth from one shoulder to the other.

How high is the sky?

The sky is part of an invisible skin of air around the Earth. This skin is called the atmosphere, and it reaches out into space for about 300 miles (500 km).

There's a very important gas called oxygen in the atmosphere — we all need to breathe oxygen to stay alive.

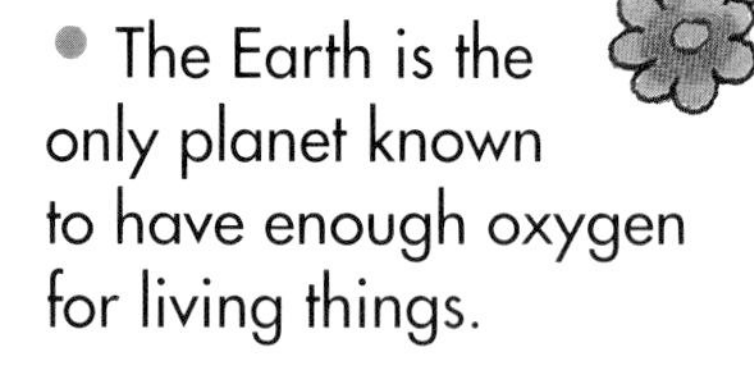

• The Earth is the only planet known to have enough oxygen for living things.

• If the Earth gets too hot, the ice at the Poles could melt. The seas would rise and drown many towns along the coasts.

What is the greenhouse effect?

The greenhouse effect is the name scientists have given to a hot problem. Waste gases from factories, power stations, and cars are building up in the atmosphere and trapping too much heat close to the Earth. Our planet may be getting warmer — like a greenhouse in summer.

3 Above the planes is the ozone layer. This works a bit like a sunblock, protecting us from the Sun's burning rays.

2 Planes fly in the next layer, high above the clouds where the skies are clear. The air is thinner here, and has less oxygen in it.

1 The atmosphere is made up of different layers. In the lowest layer, the air carries clouds and weather around the Earth.

What are clouds made of?

Some clouds look like they're made of cotton wool – but they're not! Clouds are made of billions of water droplets and ice crystals. These are so tiny and light that they float in the air.

- You'd need your umbrella on Mount Wai-'ale-'ale in Hawaii. It rains there for 350 days each year.

- Without rain, no plants would grow. Then what would we all eat?

When does rain fall from clouds?

Rain falls when water droplets in a cloud start joining together. They get bigger and heavier until, in the end, they are too heavy to float, and fall to the ground as rain.

• Have you ever heard of showers of frogs or fish? Well, they do happen. The animals are sometimes sucked up from ponds by extra-strong winds. Later on, they fall to the ground with the rain.

How cold is snow?

Snowflakes are water droplets that have frozen into crystals of ice. To stay frozen, they have to be at freezing point – that's 0 °C. If they get any warmer than this, snowflakes melt and fall to the ground as rain.

• The biggest snowman ever built was more than 22 metres high. That's about as tall as a seven-storey building.

Where do thunderstorms start?

Thunderstorms start in the huge black thunderclouds that sometimes gather at the end of a hot summer's day. Inside the clouds, strong winds hurl the water droplets around, and the cloud crackles with electricity. It flashes through the sky in great dazzling sparks, which we call lightning.

- It's safest to stay inside during a thunderstorm. Never take shelter under a tree — it might get struck by lightning.

- One man was struck by lightning seven different times! Roy C. Sullivan had his hair set alight twice and his eyebrows burned off. He even lost a big toenail.

- Lightning can travel as far as 87,000 miles (140,000 km) in 1 second!

• To find out how far away a storm is, count the number of seconds between the lightning and the thunder. The storm is 1 mile (1.6 km) away for every 5 seconds you count.

• The biggest thunderclouds tower 10 miles (16 km) into the air. That's nearly twice the height of Mount Everest.

What is thunder?

Sparks of lightning are incredibly hot. As they flash through the sky, they heat the air so quickly that it makes a loud booming noise like an explosion. This is thunder.

What is a tornado?

A tornado is a spinning twist of wind which speeds across the ground, sucking up everything in its path. Tornadoes happen mainly in North America.

Hurricanes are another kind of spinning storm, but they begin over warm tropical seas. Hurricane winds can blow at speeds of up to 240 kilometres per hour.

• In the USA, in 1931, a tornado lifted a train into the air and dumped it in a ditch.

• Air is invisible, so you can't see the wind. But you can feel it on your face, and see how it makes the trees sway.

Why does the wind blow?

When you feel the wind blow, it's because air is on the move. Air moves when it's warm. It gets lighter and it rises up into the sky. Cooler air then rushes in to take its place, making a breeze.

• Here's proof that warm air rises. Put a feather over a hot radiator and watch it float upwards on the rising air.

How big is the ocean?

The ocean is truly ENORMOUS! It covers more than twice as much of the Earth as land does. In fact, it's made up of four oceans—the Pacific, the Atlantic, the Indian, and the Arctic. Although these all have different names, they flow into each other to make one huge world ocean.

Don't go for a swim in the Arctic Ocean. It is the coldest ocean, and for most of the year it's covered in ice.

Which is the biggest ocean?

The Pacific is by far the biggest ocean in the world. It's larger than the other three oceans put together, and it's also much deeper. If you look at a globe, you'll see that the Pacific reaches halfway around the world.

• These drops of water show the oceans in order of size.

Pacific

Atlantic

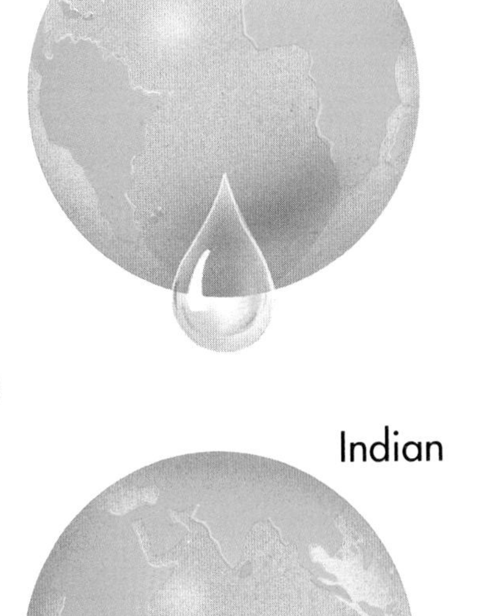

Indian

Arctic

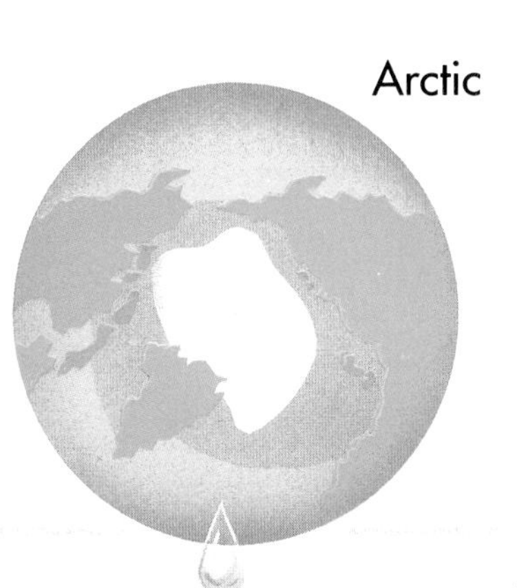

What's the difference between a sea and an ocean?

People often use the words sea and ocean to mean the same thing. That's fine, but to a scientist, seas are just part of an ocean—the parts that are nearest to land. The Mediterranean Sea is between Africa and Europe, for example.

What makes waves roll?

• Make your own waves in a bowl of water. The harder you blow across the surface, the bigger the waves.

Waves are ripples of water blown across the surface of the ocean by the wind. On a calm day they hardly move, but in stormy weather they roll faster and faster, and grow higher and higher, until they form huge walls of water.

• Some waves are called white horses because their curly white tips look like horses' manes.

• At Waimea Bay, Hawaii, surfers ride waves up to 10 metres high – that's six times taller than a man!

SCIENCE AND THE HUMAN BODY

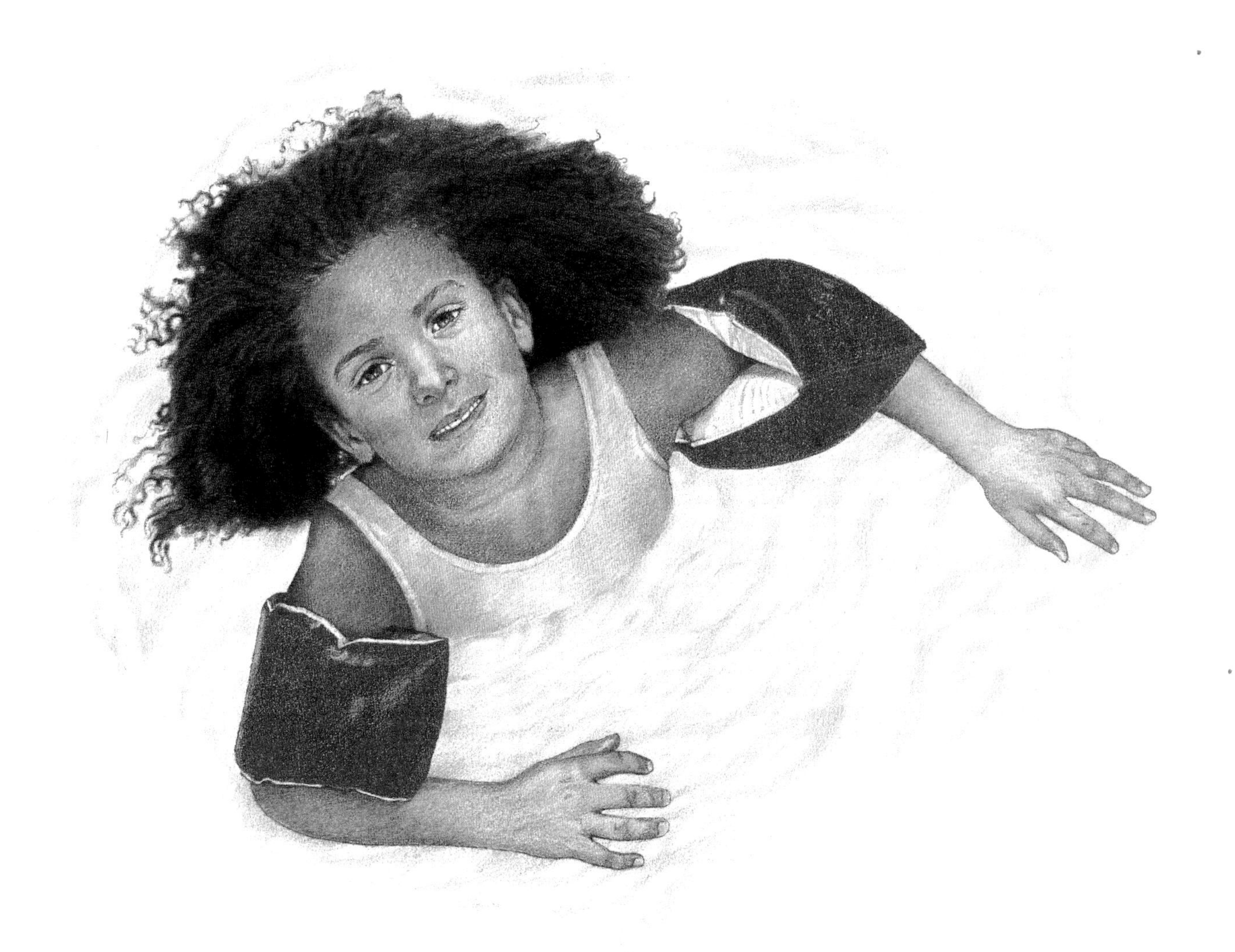

What is science about?

Science is all about discovering how and why things happen in the world around you. It's about everyday things like finding out where water goes when it boils, as well as more complicated things like why we need water to live.

3 Put some water in the freezer and leave it for an hour or two. What do you notice when you take it out? The water isn't liquid any more — it's a solid, and you can't pour solids.

2 Now fill a jug with water and pour it into a cup. Most liquids will pour, but some move faster than others. Try pouring some honey into a saucer — does it move as quickly as water?

1 The kitchen is a great place for scientists. Start by turning on a faucet and looking at the water that flows out. Runny things like water are called liquids.

What do scientists do?

One of the first things scientists do is to ask questions. Then they try to answer the questions by looking closely at things and testing out their ideas. We call this experimenting. Scientists sometimes manage to come up with the answers — but not always!

4 All liquids can change shape, but most solids can't. Pour some water into a jelly mold and it will fill up all the nooks and crannies. What happens when you put ice cubes in?

5 Ask a grown-up to put a cup of water into a saucepan and boil it for you for 5 minutes. Lots of steam comes off, doesn't it? Let the water cool, then pour it back into the cup. There's less water now — where has the rest gone?

6 When water boils, it changes from a liquid into a gas called water vapor. We can't see this gas, so it looks as though the water has disappeared.

Why do I run out of energy?

• When you run, the stored energy in your body is changed into movement energy.

You run out of energy because you use it! Walking, running and jumping all need energy – without it you wouldn't be able to talk, write, read or even sleep! Energy is stored inside your body and comes from your food. That's why you get hungry – your body is telling you to put back some of the energy you've used.

• Lots of things give out energy, in many different forms. Here are just some of them.

Fire = heat energy

Bike = movement energy

Drum = sound energy

• Eating a small apple gives you enough energy to sleep for half an hour.

• Energy is never made or destroyed. It just changes from one form to another. Bending a bow stores energy in the bow. This changes into movement energy as the arrow flies from the bow.

What is energy?

Energy makes things happen – nothing in the universe would work without it. You can't see energy, but you can see what it does to things around you. Because of energy, cars move and planes fly, lamps give out light, drums make music, and fires give off heat.

Food = chemical energy

Train = electrical energy

Torch = light energy

Why does the spoon get hot when I stir my cocoa?

Heat energy never stays still. It is always moving. The teaspoon warms up when you stir your cocoa because heat energy is moving from the hot drink into the spoon.

• Things that allow heat to pass through them easily are called conductors. A metal spoon is a good conductor.

• Our bodies give off heat all the time. Some burglar alarms work by picking up the heat given off by a burglar's body.

Why is sunlight warm?

Sunlight is warm because the Sun gives off heat as well as light energy. The Sun's heat energy travels toward us in invisible straight lines called heat rays. You can't see them, of course, but you can feel them on your skin on hot sunny days.

• You get cold feet when you stand on a tiled floor because the tiles carry heat energy away from them. Your feet feel warmer on a carpet because it doesn't carry heat away as well as the tiles do.

How do hang gliders hitch lifts?

When the Sun heats the land, the land then warms the air above it. Warm air is lighter than cold air, and it rises up into the sky. Hang gliders use this rising warm air to help them to fly. The rising currents of warm air are called thermals.

What is sound?

Sound is a type of energy. It happens when something shakes or moves back and forwards really quickly. The shaking movements are called vibrations. You hear sounds because vibrations travel through the air into your ears.

• Some singers can sing a note which is so high and so loud that it breaks a glass!

• Here's a way to see how sounds vibrate. Tie a piece of thread to some tissue paper. Now, put on some loud music and hold the thread in front of a loud-speaker. The vibrations should make the tissue paper shake. If they don't, turn up the music!

• Crashing a pair of cymbals together makes them vibrate, sending out ringing sounds.

Why do trumpeters blow raspberries?

Blowing raspberries is the only way to get sounds out of a trumpet! It makes a trumpeter's lips vibrate, and this makes the air inside the trumpet shake, too. The air comes out the other end as a musical note!

• Sound travels through air at 340 metres per second. That's nearly the length of four football pitches.

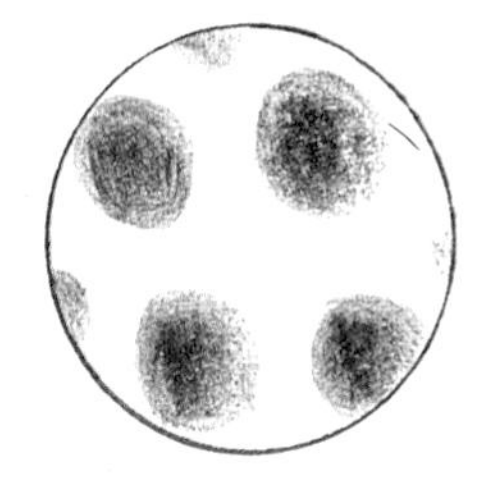

Can sound travel under water?

• Sound needs something to travel through – air, water, or some other material. There's no air in space, so astronauts have to use radios to talk to one another.

Yes, it can! Sound moves four times faster through water than through air. It can travel such long distances that whales can hear each other when they are over a hundred kilometres apart.

What is air made of?

Air is a mixture of gases — mostly nitrogen and oxygen, with a little bit of carbon dioxide and some water vapor. It also has tiny bits of salt, dust, and dirt. You can't see, smell, or taste the air, but you can feel it when the wind blows.

• You're using air when you take a deep breath and blow out the candles on a cake!

• We don't notice it, but the air around us is heavy, and pushes down on us. The air in a medium-sized room weighs as much as 70 cans of baked beans!

How do bubbles get into fizzy drinks?

The bubbles in carbonated drinks are carbon dioxide gas. The gas is squashed into the bottle so hard that it disappears into the drink. When the bottle is opened, the bubbles have room to escape and start fizzing.

• Make your own bubbles of carbon dioxide gas by adding a teaspoon of baking powder to a cup of water. Stand by for the fizz!

Why do cakes rise?

When you put a cake in the oven, the mixture heats up and makes bubbles of carbon dioxide. These grow bigger in the heat, and make the cake rise.

• The air you beat into a cake mixture also helps to make the cake deliciously light.

Why do shadows happen?

Light travels in straight lines called rays. When the rays hit something that they can't shine through, the light is blocked, and a dark shadow forms on the other side.

• Try to make animal shadows on a wall by wiggling your fingers in the beam of a bright torch.

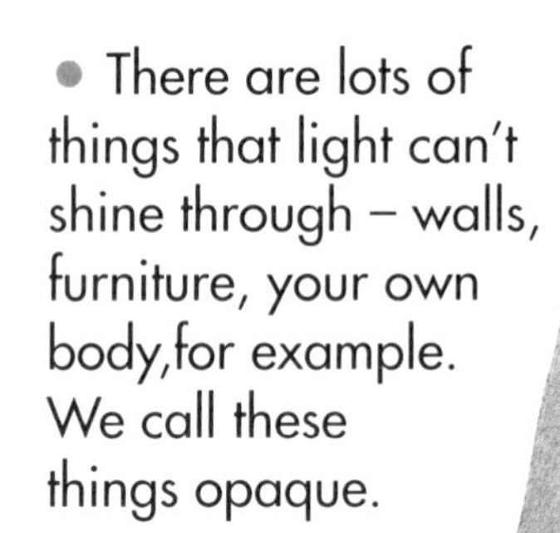

• There are lots of things that light can't shine through – walls, furniture, your own body,for example. We call these things opaque.

• Light is another kind of energy. Plants use the energy in sunlight to make food for themselves in their leaves. Sunflowers get all the sunlight they can by turning to face the Sun as it moves across the sky.

• Did you know that you can use shadows to tell the time? Next time it's sunny, stand a pencil inside a thread spool on a piece of paper. Every hour, draw a line along the pencil's shadow, and write down the time. Now you can use your shadow clock to tell the time on every sunny day.

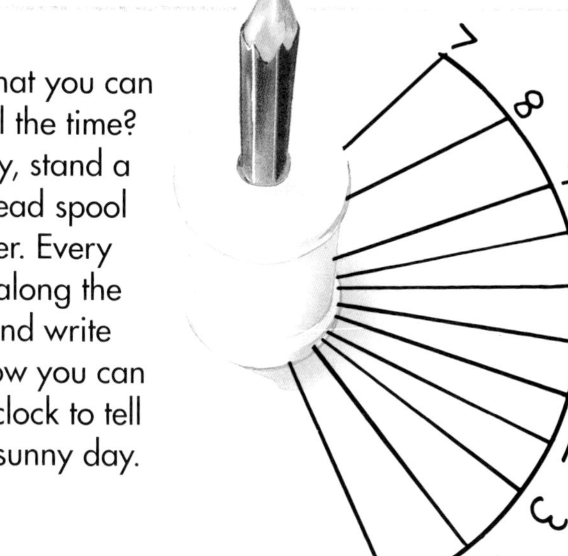

Why can I see through glass?

You can see through glass because it's transparent — that means it's clear, and it lets the light shine through. Glass is great for windows because it lets sunlight into a room, and allows you to see what's going on in the world outside!

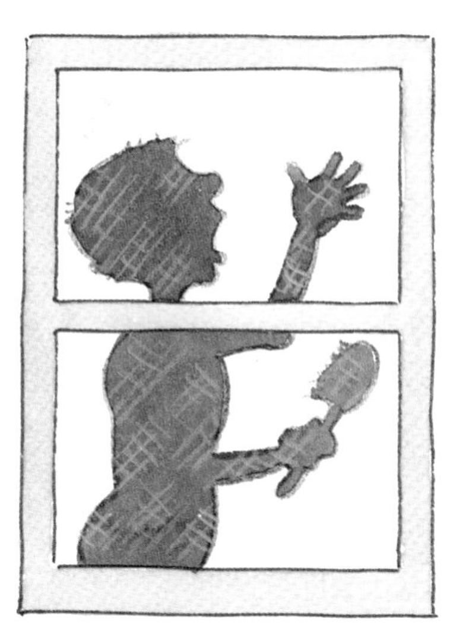

• Bathroom windows are often made of frosted glass. This still lets some light through, but the frosting stops people from seeing straight through the glass.

Can light bounce?

When rays of light hit something that they can't shine through, they bounce off it — just like a ball bouncing. This is called reflection. We are able to see things because light is reflected off them into our eyes.

• You can see yourself when you look down into a puddle because the smooth water reflects the light straight back into your eyes.

• Up periscope! A submarine officer looks through a periscope to see what's happening above the water. Mirrors inside the periscope reflect light from things above the water straight down into the officer's eyes.

• The Moon reflects light from the Sun. It has no light of its own.

• See what happens when light passes through a single drop of water. Cut a hole in a piece of cardboard and stick clear tape over the top. Carefully put a drop of water on the tape and look through it at something small, like a ladybug. It will make it look bigger.

Why do my legs look shorter under water?

When light enters water, its rays travel more slowly than they do through the air. This changes the way we see things. Looking down through the water in a swimming pool, your legs look very short and dumpy. Don't worry — they aren't really!

• As light passes through water, it changes the way we see things. This makes it tricky to net fish — they aren't where they appear to be. To catch one, you have to aim below the place where you actually see it.

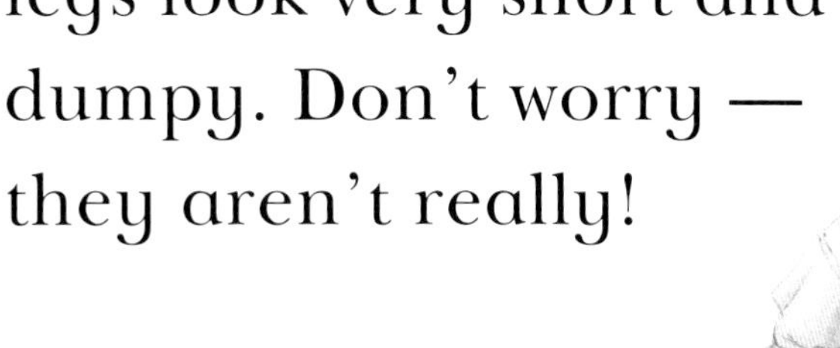

Why do rainbows happen?

Although sunlight looks white, it's really made up of lots of different colors. During a shower of rain, the Sun sometimes shines through the tiny raindrops that fall through the air. When this happens, the water makes the light spread into all its different colors. The colors always appear in the same order, and a beautiful rainbow forms in the sky.

Cardboard

Flashlight = beam

Reflected light

Mirror

• Another way to see a rainbow is to hold a mirror in a shallow dish of water. Try to bounce sunlight off the mirror onto a piece of white cardboard. The water should make the light spread out into a rainbow.

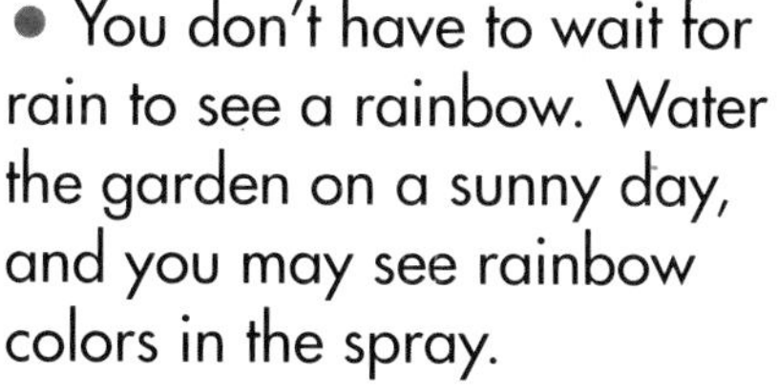

• You don't have to wait for rain to see a rainbow. Water the garden on a sunny day, and you may see rainbow colors in the spray.

Why is grass green?

We see things when light reflects off them into our eyes. But not all of white light's colors are reflected. Some are soaked up. Grass looks green because it soaks up all the colors in white light apart from green.

• The bright colors of many animals often work as a warning. The black and yellow stripes on a wasp warn us — and other animals — to keep away from its poisonous sting.

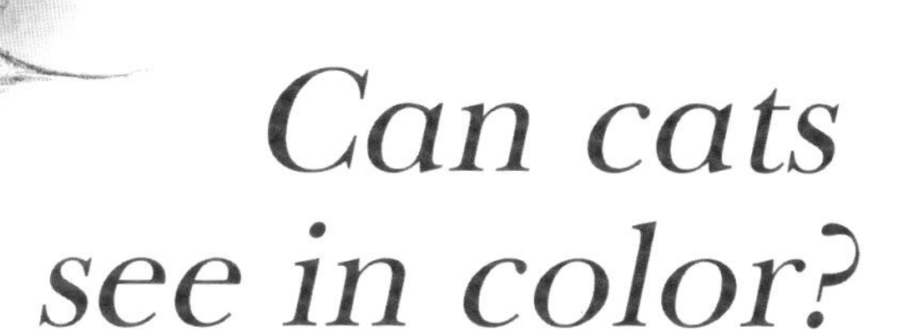

Can cats see in color?

• Many animals don't really need to see in color. They rely far more on their sharp hearing and sense of smell.

Yes, they can — but they don't see all the colors that you do! Cats don't need to see bright colors, as most of them are busiest at night, outdoors hunting for food.

What can walk on water?

Tiny insects called water striders are so light that they can walk across water without sinking into it! But even water striders wouldn't get anywhere without a force called surface tension. This pulls on the surface of the water, making a thin stretchy "skin" on the top.

Raindrops aren't quite round — they're almost flat underneath.

Why are water droplets round?

Small drops of water are almost perfectly round because they are pulled into this shape by surface tension. Bigger drops spread out, though — they're too heavy for surface tension to work so well.

• The Jesus Christ lizard runs so fast that it can cross rivers and lakes without sinking — a brilliant way to escape from danger!

• Gently touch a drop of water with a soapy straw, and see how the drop gets flatter. This is because soap weakens the surface tension of water — it can no longer pull the drop into a neat round shape.

Why does soap make bubbles?

Adding soap to water weakens the pull of the surface tension and makes the surface of the water much stretchier. It spreads out enough for you to blow air inside — it's a bit like blowing up balloons.

Why do we need air?

All the animals on Earth need to breathe oxygen to stay alive — and that includes you! That's because bodies use oxygen to make energy for living.

- All plants need air, light, and water to live and grow. So do people, and every living thing on our planet.

- Even though they live in the sea, whales breathe oxygen from the air. Sperm whales can hold their breath for up to two hours before coming up for air.

Why do we need light?

Without the Sun's light, there would be nothing to eat! Plants are the only living things that can make their own food, and they need sunlight to do this. Everything else on Earth feeds on plants, or on plant-eating animals. If there weren't any plants, we'd all starve to death!

• If you've ever been camping, you'll know that the grass beneath a tent goes pale and begins to die. This is because it can't get the sunlight it needs to stay alive. Don't worry, it soon recovers!

Why do we need water?

It's hard to imagine, but more than two-thirds of your body is made of water. And the same is true for most other animals and plants. All of the living things on Earth need water to stay alive. Without it, they would die.

• You can survive for many weeks without food. But without water you'd last just three or four days.

Where do I come from?

You began when a tiny egg inside your mother (no bigger than a period) joined with a tiny bit of your father, called a sperm. Then you grew and grew until you were big enough to be born.

• You stayed in your mother's uterus for about nine months. As you got bigger, her uterus stretched to make space for you.

Uterus

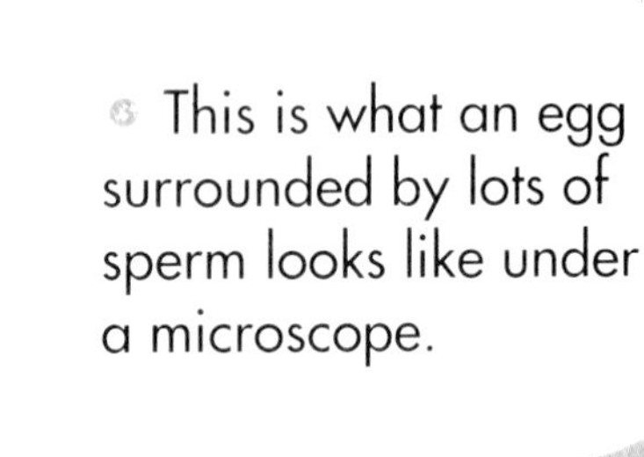

• This is what an egg surrounded by lots of sperm looks like under a microscope.

Uterus

• In the uterus, you floated in a kind of bag filled with water which kept you safe and warm.

• You grew inside your mother in a part of her body called the uterus, or womb.

• When you were ready to be born, the opening of your mother's uterus stretched to let you out.

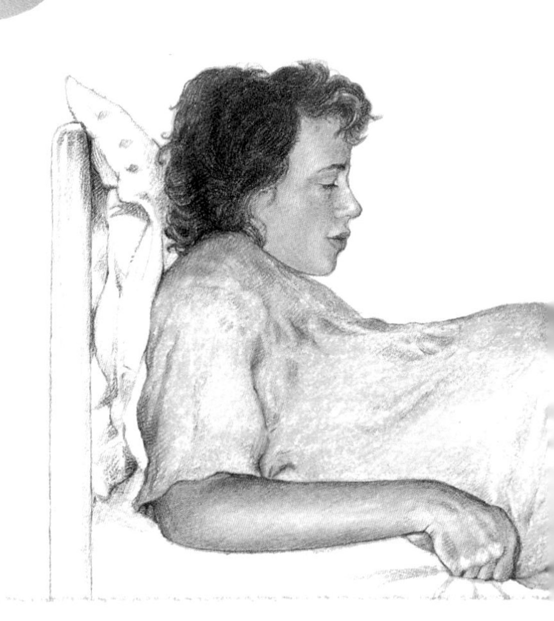

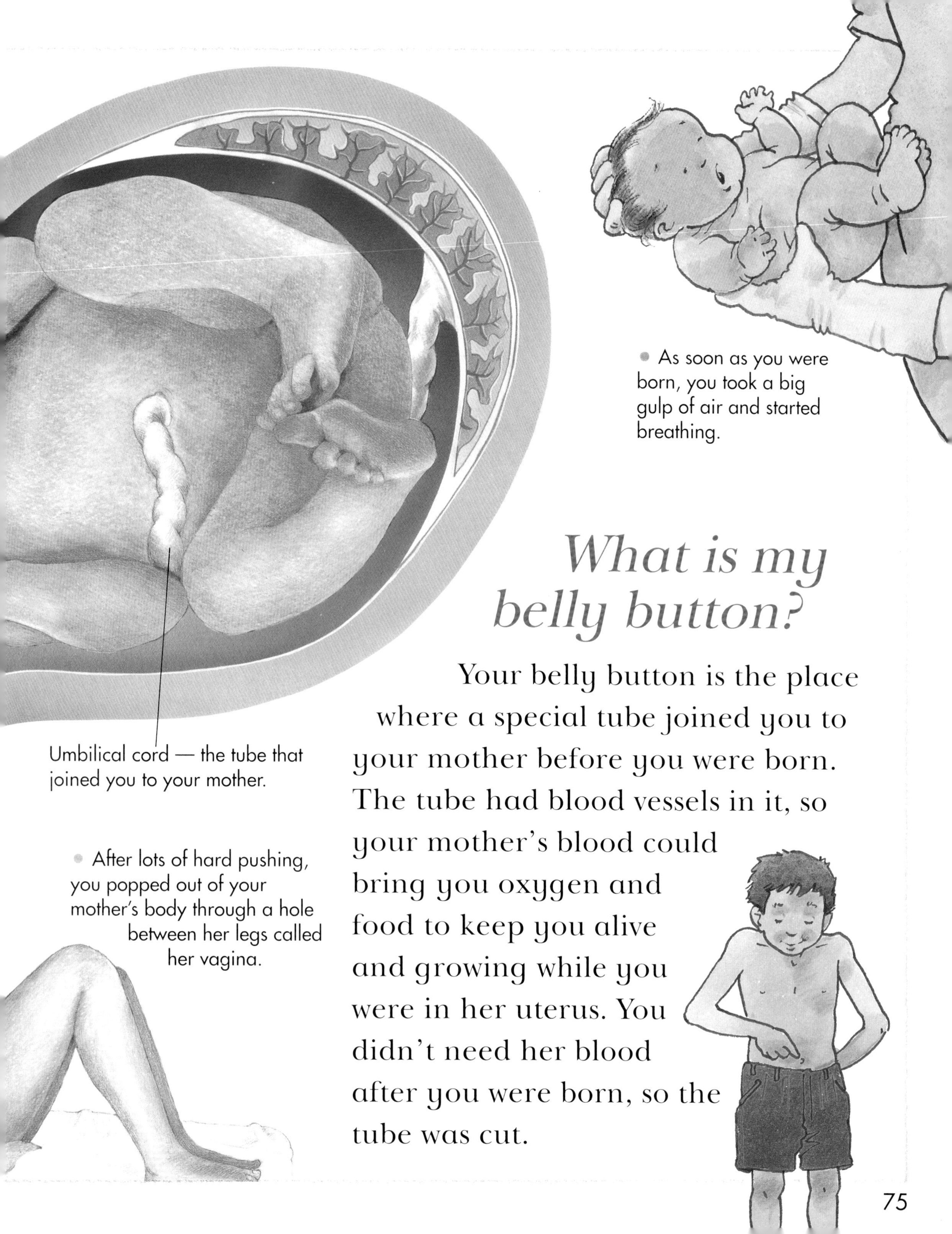

As soon as you were born, you took a big gulp of air and started breathing.

What is my belly button?

Your belly button is the place where a special tube joined you to your mother before you were born. The tube had blood vessels in it, so your mother's blood could bring you oxygen and food to keep you alive and growing while you were in her uterus. You didn't need her blood after you were born, so the tube was cut.

Umbilical cord — the tube that joined you to your mother.

After lots of hard pushing, you popped out of your mother's body through a hole between her legs called her vagina.

How many bones do I have?

When you were born, you had more than 300 bones. But by the time you finish growing, you will have just over 200!

The missing bones won't have fallen out or disappeared. Instead, as you get older, some of your smaller bones will join together to make bigger ones.

• Without bones inside you to give you a shape, you'd be like a floppy, squishy bag.

Thighbone

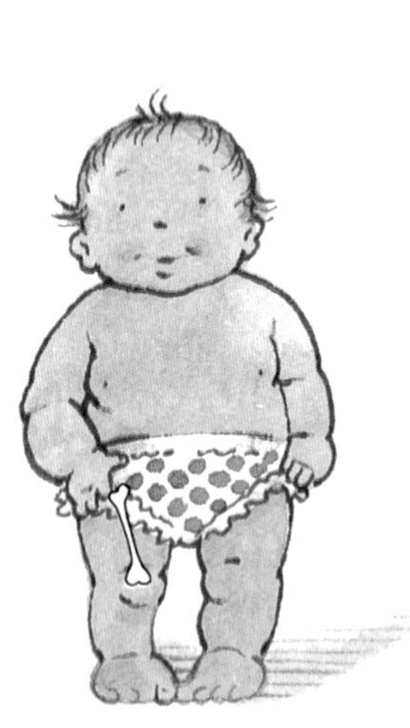

• The longest bone in your body is the one above your knee, called your thighbone.

• Your bones are partly made of hard stony stuff called calcium, but unlike stones they are alive. They get bigger as you grow up.

Foot bones

• Most of us have twelve pairs of ribs, but some people have an extra one. Your ribs help to keep your lungs and heart safe.

• Although your skull is made of lots of bones, most of them are fixed in place. Only your jawbone moves.

• Bones are hard and strong. They help to keep the softer parts inside you (like your brain) from getting hurt.

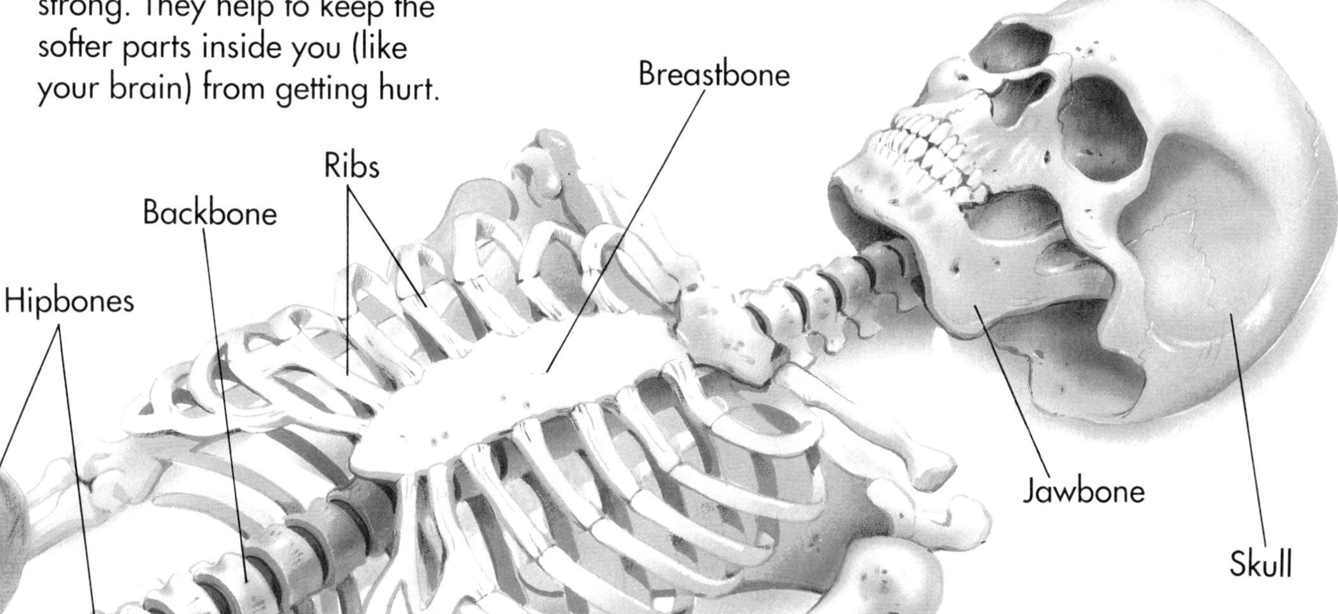

What is my funny bone?

The funny thing about your funny bone is that it isn't a bone at all. It's a nerve that runs just under your skin over each elbow. If you bang your elbow, the nerve is banged, too. It sends a message to your brain and you feel pain!

How do I move?

Muscles make you move, by pulling your bones around. When you smile or cry, speak or eat, walk or skip, muscles are doing the work.

• A muscle can only make itself shorter. It needs another muscle pulling the other way to stretch it out again.

• Your biggest muscles are the ones you sit on!

Why do strong people have big muscles?

Muscles get bigger and stronger if they are used a lot. That's why athletes practice hard and do lots of exercises.

• Many tennis players have bigger muscles in the arm they use to hold their racket.

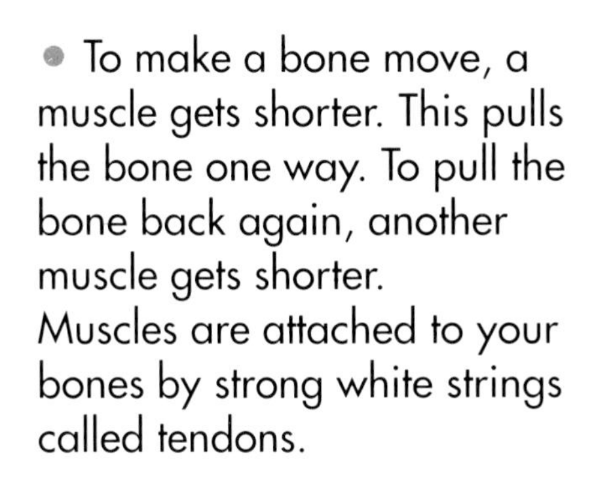
• To make a bone move, a muscle gets shorter. This pulls the bone one way. To pull the bone back again, another muscle gets shorter. Muscles are attached to your bones by strong white strings called tendons.

Tendon

This muscle tightens to bend your arm.

When this muscle tightens, your arm straightens.

What is a cramp?

A cramp is when a muscle suddenly feels tight and painful. It stops moving properly and it feels as if it's stuck. No one is quite sure why a cramp happens, but it goes away if you rest the sore spot. Rubbing it can also help.

• Have you ever had a stitch after running? It's a pain in your side, just under your ribs. It means you have a cramp in the breathing muscle below your lungs.

What does my heart do?

Your heart is a very special muscle which keeps blood moving around your body. If you put your hand on your chest near your heart, you'll feel it beating. Each time it beats, it pumps blood out around your body.

• To hear a heart beating, find somewhere quiet and rest your ear against a friend's chest. You should hear two sounds close together.— "lub-dub, lub-dub."

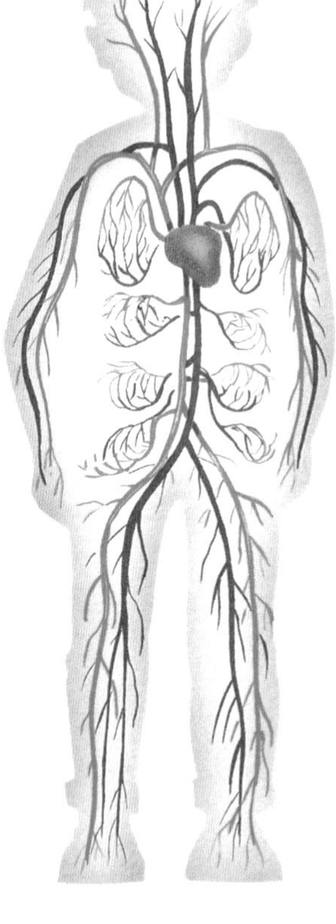

• Blood travels around your body in thin tubes called blood vessels.

• Your body is using up oxygen all the time, keeping you alive, so it has to keep getting more from your lungs.

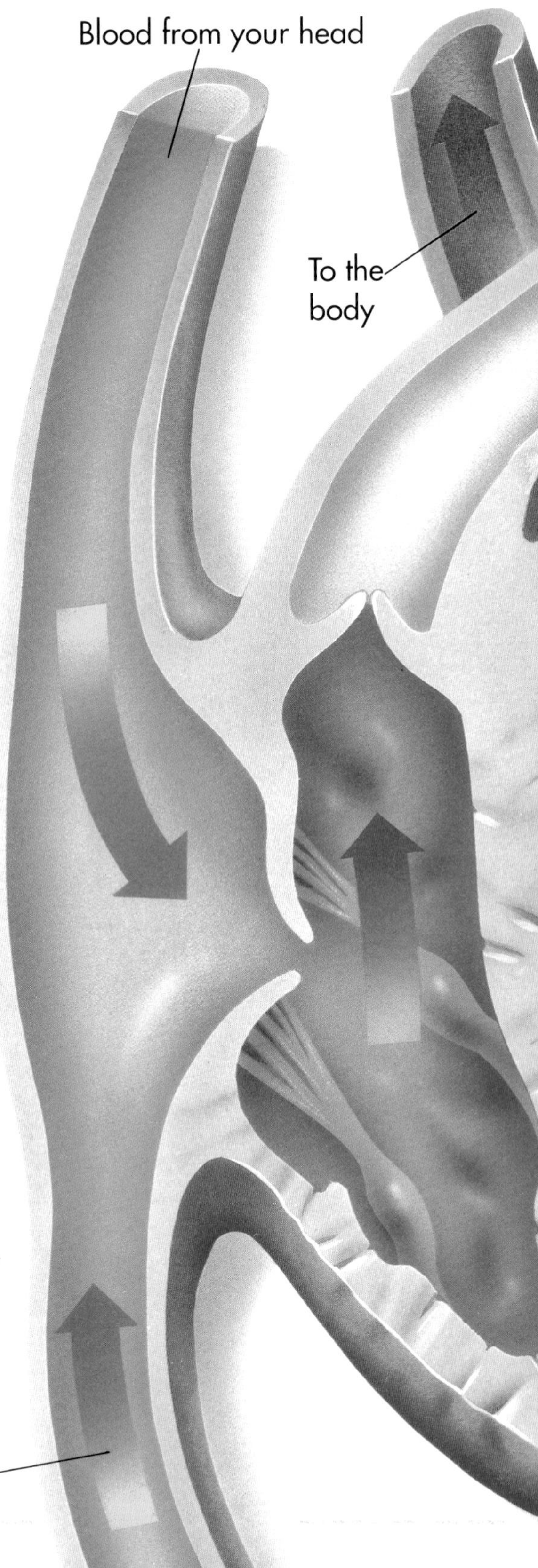

• One side of your heart pumps blood to your lungs to get oxygen. The other side pumps it around your body.

What is blood for?

• Some insects have blue or green blood.

Your blood is like a fast-moving river flowing around your body. It carries useful things — like oxygen from the air you breathe, and the goodness from the food you eat — to every part of you. It also helps your body to fight germs.

• When you were a baby, you had less than a quart (a liter) of blood — not quite enough to fill a milk carton. When you grow up, you will have about 5 quarts (5 liters) of blood — enough to half fill a bucket!

How big is my heart?

Our hearts grow with us — they get bigger as we do. Whatever size you are now, your heart will be a bit bigger than your fist.

What is inside my head?

The most exciting and important part of your body is hidden inside your head, beneath your hair, your skin, and your hard skull bone. It is your brain.

Your brain is the part of you that thinks and remembers. It also makes sure the rest of your body is doing what it should!

• Your brain has two sides. The right side of your brain takes care of the left side of your body, while the left side takes care of the right side of your body.

• People's brains come in different sizes. But bigger brains don't make people smarter — any more than having big feet makes them better runners!

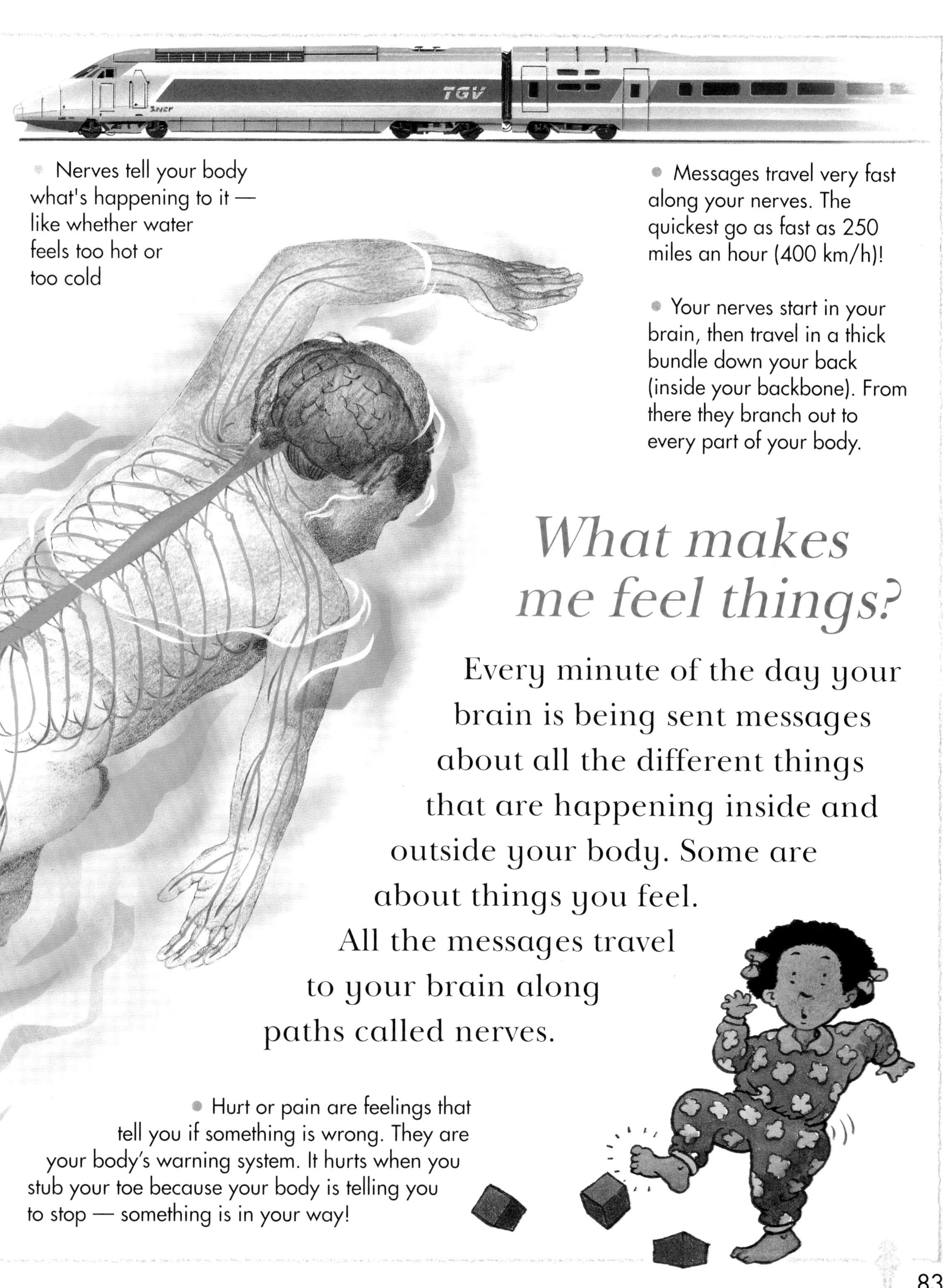

• Nerves tell your body what's happening to it — like whether water feels too hot or too cold

• Messages travel very fast along your nerves. The quickest go as fast as 250 miles an hour (400 km/h)!

• Your nerves start in your brain, then travel in a thick bundle down your back (inside your backbone). From there they branch out to every part of your body.

What makes me feel things?

Every minute of the day your brain is being sent messages about all the different things that are happening inside and outside your body. Some are about things you feel. All the messages travel to your brain along paths called nerves.

• Hurt or pain are feelings that tell you if something is wrong. They are your body's warning system. It hurts when you stub your toe because your body is telling you to stop — something is in your way!

Why do I breathe?

You pull air into your body when you breathe. And air is something your body cannot do without, even for just a few minutes.

This is because air has a gas called oxygen in it, and your body needs oxygen to live and grow.

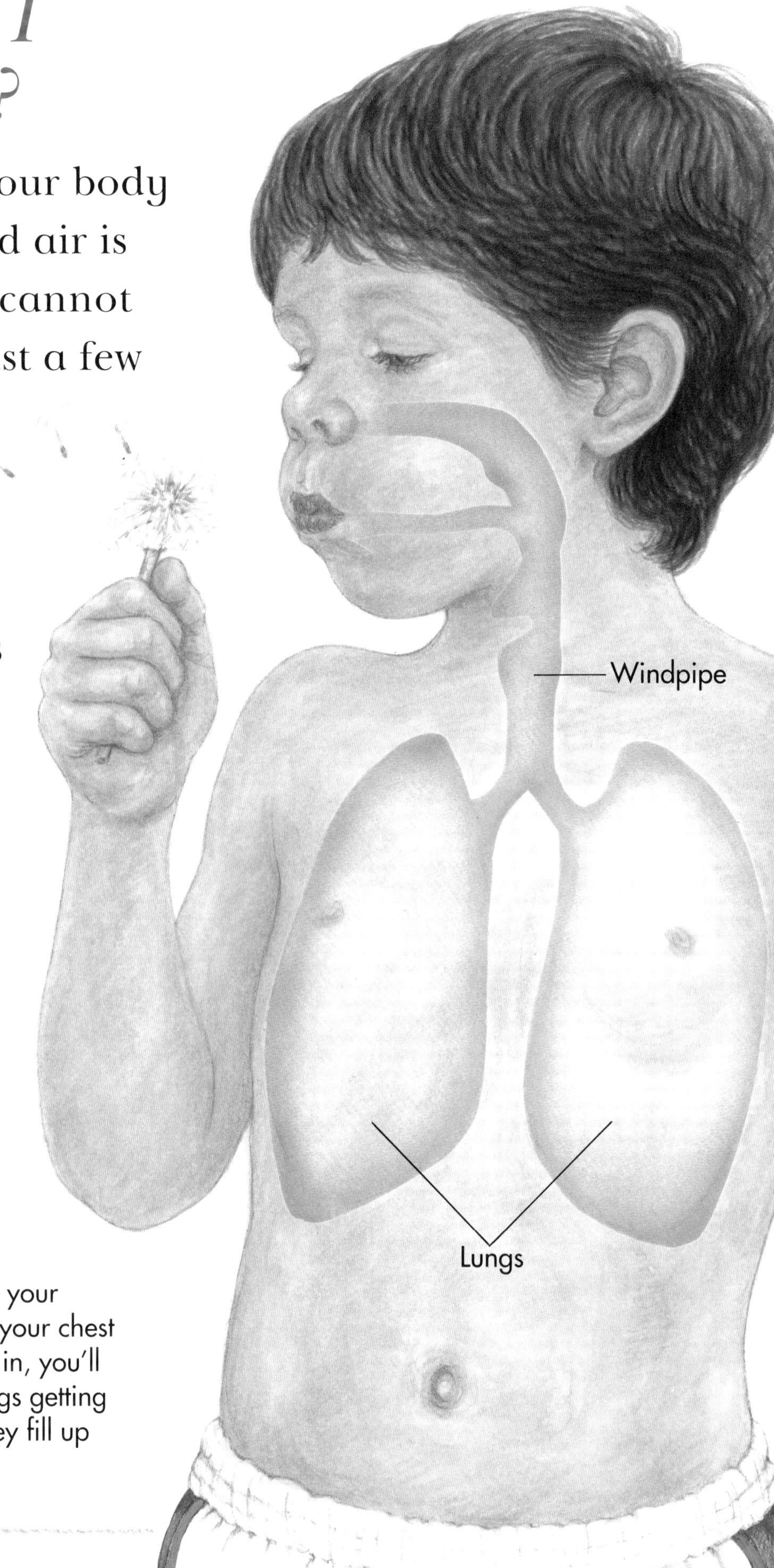

- When you breathe in, air goes down your windpipe to your lungs. These are like big sponges that hold air instead of water.

- If you fold your arms across your chest and breathe in, you'll feel your lungs getting bigger as they fill up with air.

Why do I get hiccups?

There's a big muscle below your lungs which helps you to breathe. It's called your diaphragm. You hiccup when something makes this muscle pull down really hard, drawing lots of air into your lungs. To keep too much air from rushing in, a flap at the top of your windpipe clamps down. This closes off the air flow so quickly that your whole body jerks.

• "HIC" is air rushing in.

• "CUP" is the flap clamping down over your windpipe.

What makes me sneeze?

If dust or germs get into your nose, your body makes you sneeze to get rid of them. Your lungs shoot air out, clearing your nose.

• When you sneeze, air rushes down your nose at over 100 miles an hour (160 km/h)!

Why do I blink?

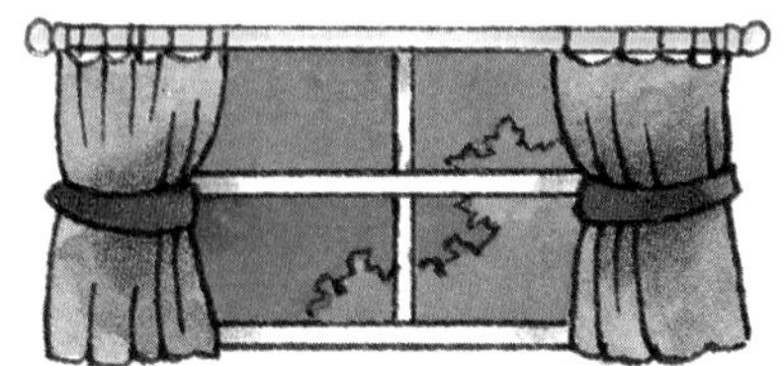

• The iris is the colored part of your eye. It works a little like curtains on a window — when it's too dark to see, the iris opens to let in more light. When the light is too bright, the iris tightens up to protect the eye.

Your eyes make tears all the time, not only when you cry. Blinking spreads the tears across your eyes and stops them from drying out and getting sore.

• A blink lasts for about one-third of a second. You do it thousands of times a day.

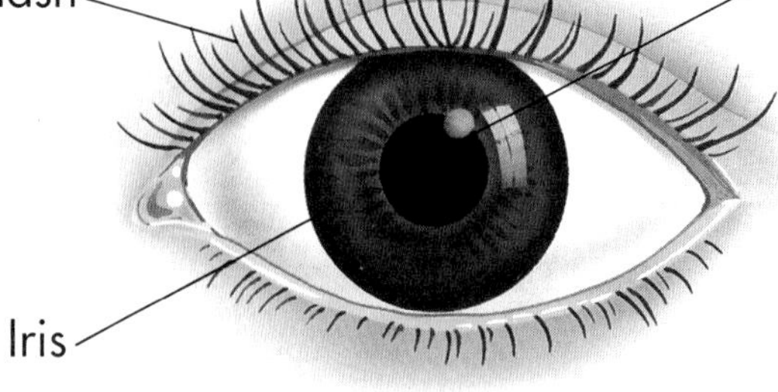

• Eyelashes help to keep things like dust and grit from getting into your eyes.

• The black hole in the middle of the eye is called the pupil.

• Jellylike stuff in your eyeball keeps it in shape, like air in a balloon.

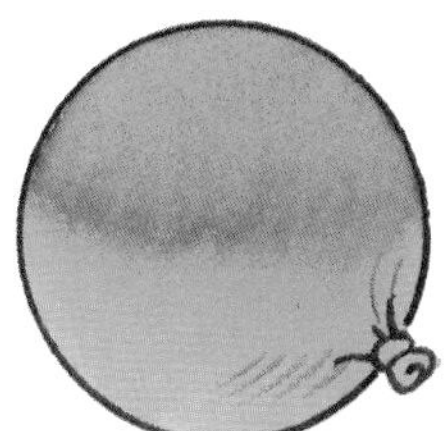

Why can't I see in the dark?

You can't see much when it's dark, because eyes need light to see. If you look at your eyes in a mirror, you'll see a black hole in the middle of them. Light bounces off everything around you and in through this hole. Messages are then sent from your eyes to your brain, telling you what you are looking at.

• The lining at the back of the eye is called the retina. The picture that forms here is upside down! Your brain turns it the right way up.

A nerve inside here carries messages to your brain.

• There's a lens at the front of the eye. It makes sure the things you see aren't fuzzy, by making light shine in the right place at the back of the eye.

Why are ears such a funny shape?

The shape of your ears helps them to catch sounds from the air. The sounds then go through your outer ear into the hidden part of your ear, inside your head. Animals like rabbits can move their ears to help them catch sounds.

Why do I feel dizzy when I spin around?

Inside each ear, you have three loop-shaped tubes with watery liquid in them. This swishes around when you spin. Special nerves pick up this movement and tell the brain you are spinning. If you stop suddenly, the liquid goes on swishing around for a little longer. Your brain gets the wrong message and you feel dizzy!

Earlobe

• Did you know that you have a drum in your ear? Your eardrum is a piece of thin skin that moves back and forth very quickly when sounds hit it.

• When your eardrum moves, it makes three tiny bones wobble.

• When the bones wobble, they make watery liquid deep inside your ear move, too. Special nerves pick up this movement and send messages to your brain.

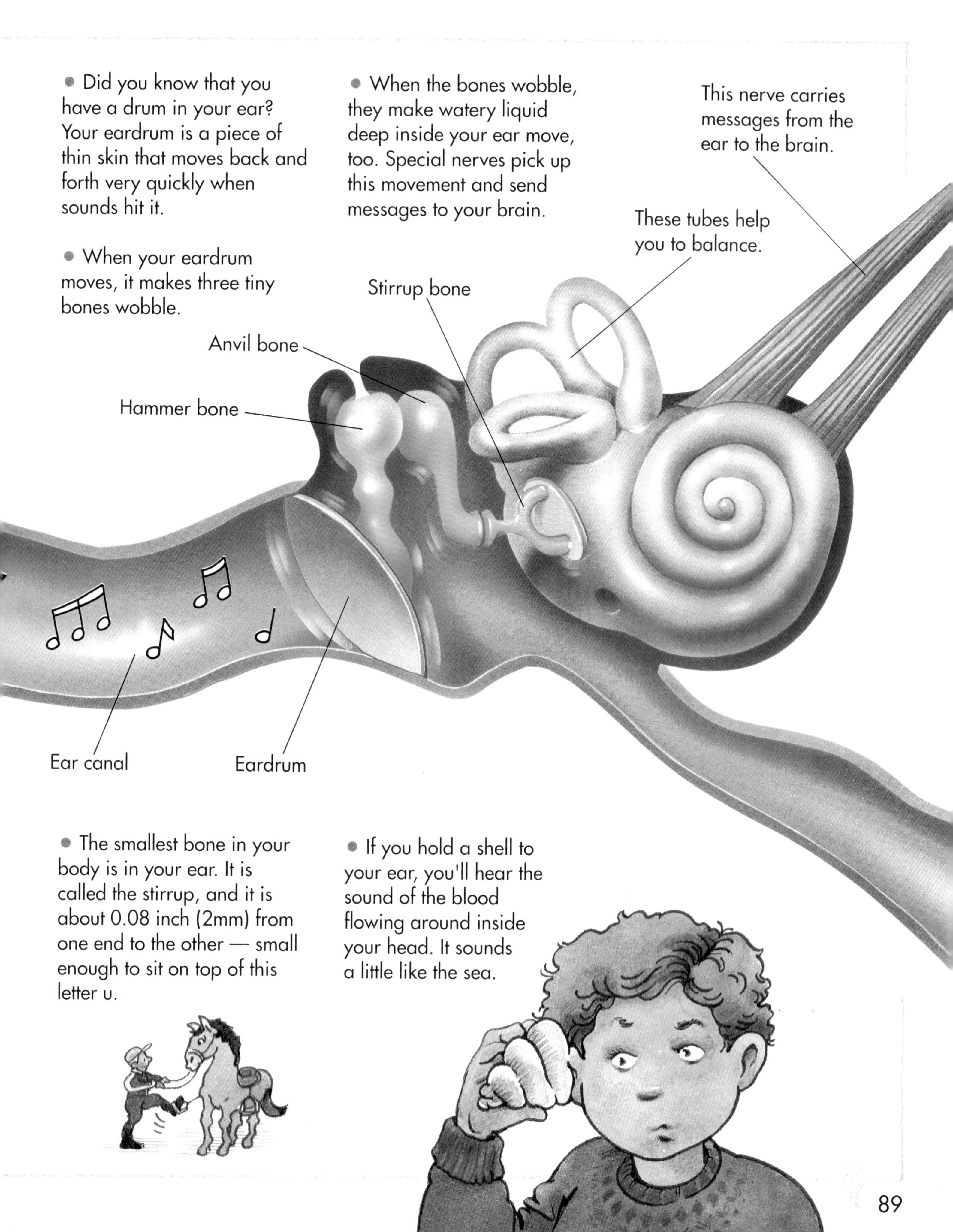

• The smallest bone in your body is in your ear. It is called the stirrup, and it is about 0.08 inch (2mm) from one end to the other — small enough to sit on top of this letter u.

• If you hold a shell to your ear, you'll hear the sound of the blood flowing around inside your head. It sounds a little like the sea.

What is my nose for?

Your nose is for smelling things, and it also helps your tongue with tasting. It can do this because tiny bits of food are carried by air up into your nose when you eat. The bits are much too small to see, but nerves inside your nose find them and send messages about them to your brain.

- When a cold stuffs up your nose, air can't get to the nose nerves and you can't taste your food properly.

- Here's a way to see how much you taste things with your nose. You'll need someone to help you.

1 Get two different flavors of fruit yogurt.

2 Shut your eyes tight and hold your nose.

3 See if you can tell which yogurt you are eating.

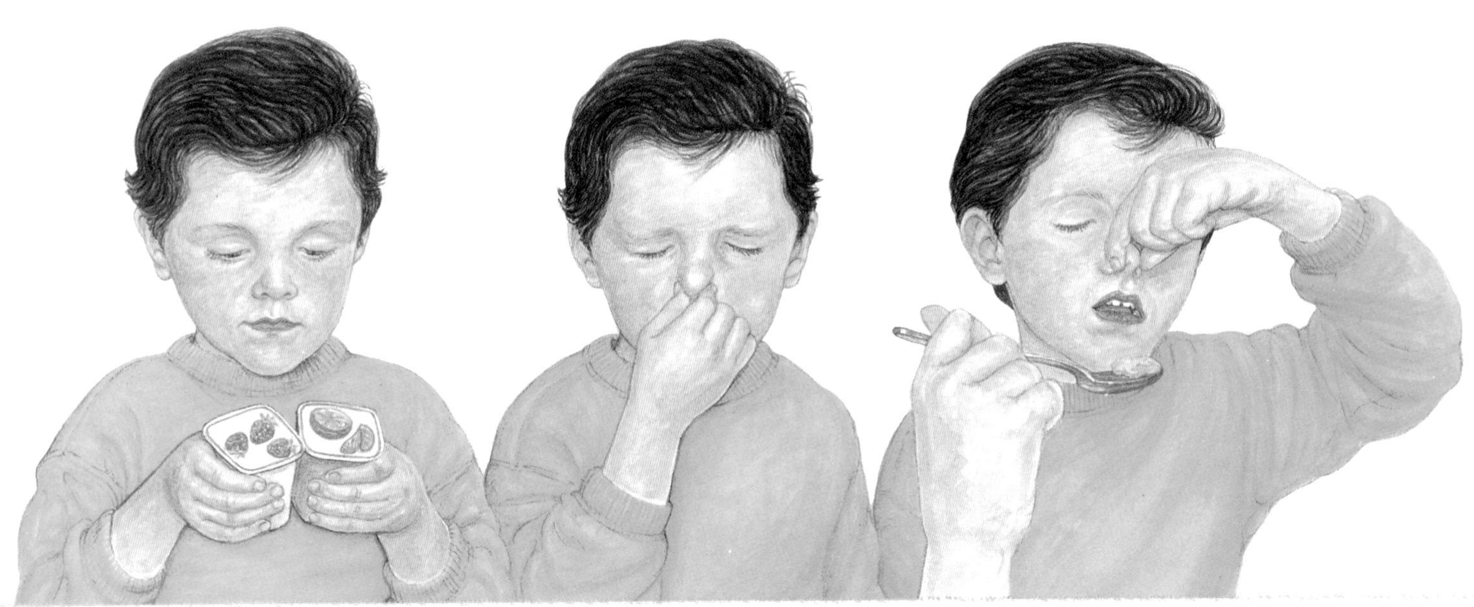

• To see how your tongue helps you to speak, put your finger on it and try to say "Hello."

What is my tongue for?

Your tongue is for tasting things, but it also helps you speak and sing. It is covered with tiny little bumps called tastebuds which send messages along nerves to your brain about the food you eat.

Why do teeth fall out?

• When you are grown up, you will have between 28 and 32 teeth.

As you grow up, most parts of your body get bigger. But your teeth can't grow bigger, and so you have to replace them.

When you are small, you have twenty small teeth called milk teeth. These start to fall out when you are five or six years old, to let new, bigger teeth grow in their place.

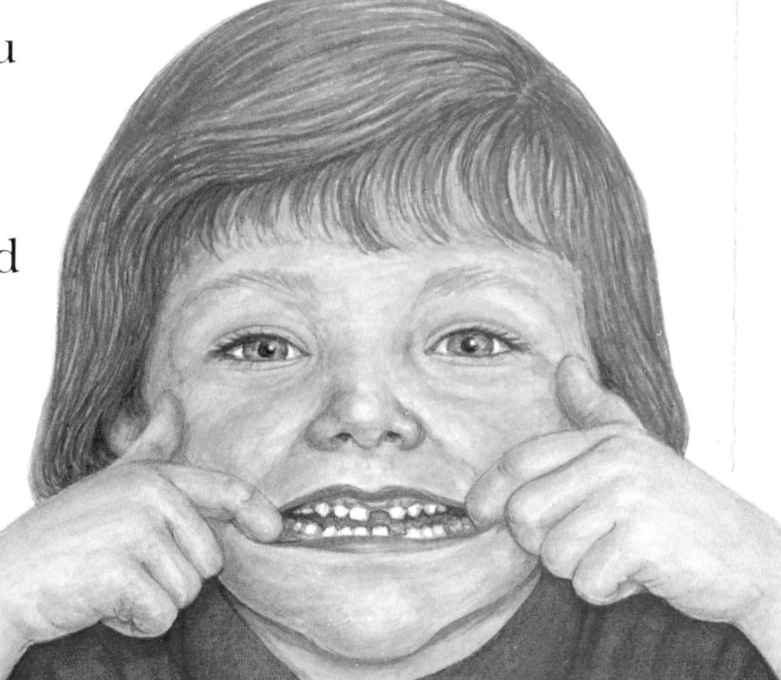

Why do I get sick sometimes?

When a part of your body stops working properly, you get sick. You don't feel right. Maybe your stomach hurts, or you may have a lot of itchy spots on your skin. Sickness often happens because things called germs get inside your body.

• Sometimes your body has to fight and kill germs. The doctor may give you medicine to help it to do this.

• Some germs like dirt. Washing your body and cleaning your teeth help to keep these germs away.

TRANSPORTATION AND BUILDINGS

How far can I go in an hour?

If you keep walking for an hour, and don't stop to take any rests, your own two legs will carry you about 2½ miles (4 km). You'll be able to go farther if you run, but you'll probably have to keep stopping to get your breath back. The easiest way to travel more than a few miles in an hour is to get something to carry you!

- It would take an ordinary garden snail more than three days to get as far as you can walk in one hour.

- Trotting on a pony for an hour, you'd be able to travel three times as far as you would on foot.

- To walk as far as a jumbo jet can carry you in an hour, you'd have to keep going for more than ten whole days and nights!

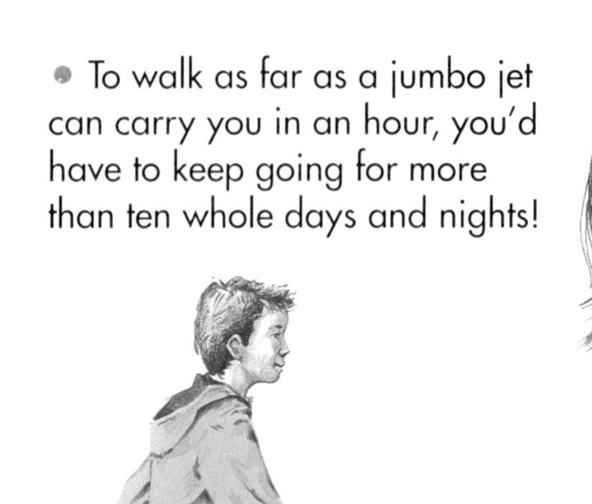

- Racing cyclists can pedal at least ten times as fast as you can walk. They can go as far as 25 miles (40 km) in an hour.

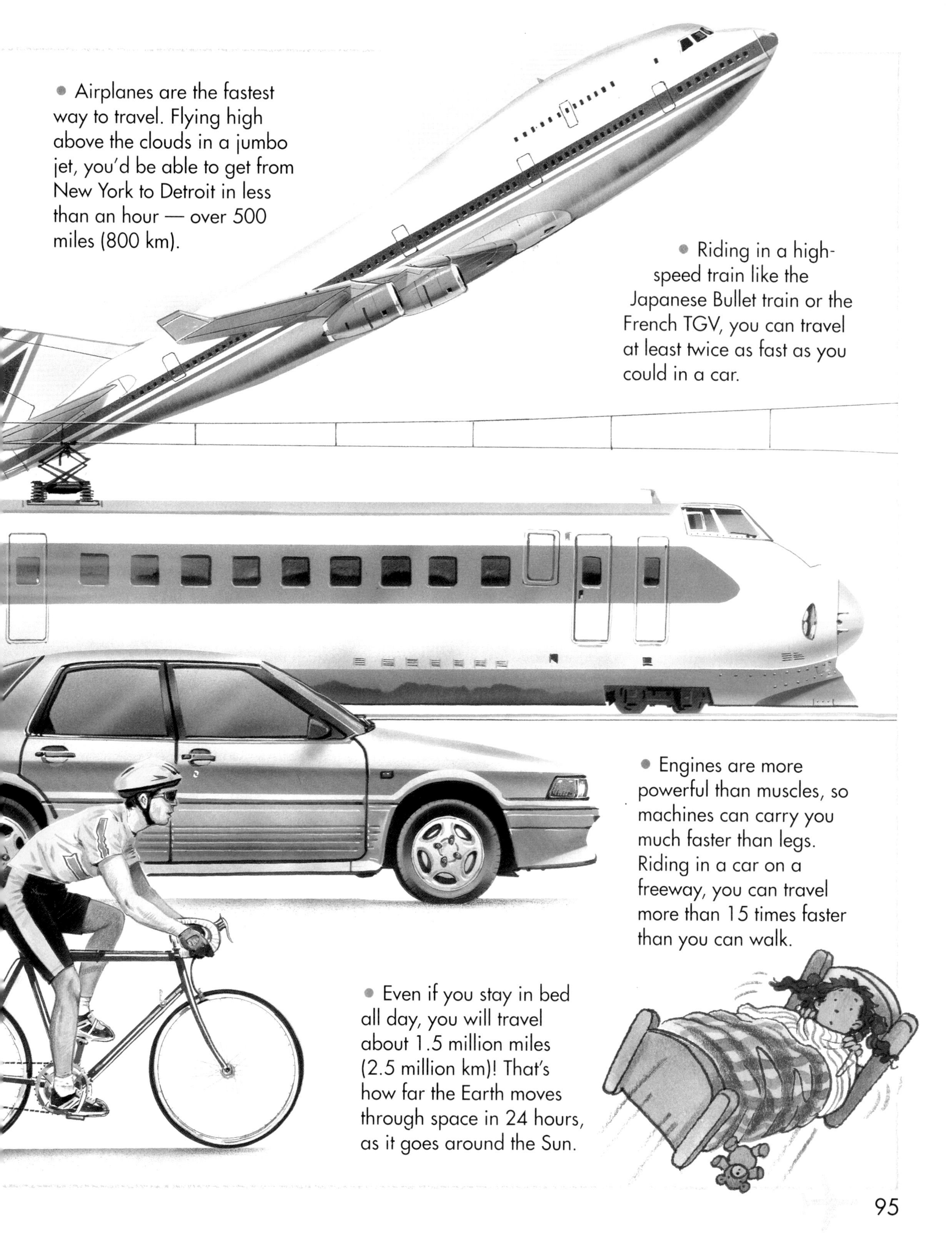

• Airplanes are the fastest way to travel. Flying high above the clouds in a jumbo jet, you'd be able to get from New York to Detroit in less than an hour — over 500 miles (800 km).

• Riding in a high-speed train like the Japanese Bullet train or the French TGV, you can travel at least twice as fast as you could in a car.

• Engines are more powerful than muscles, so machines can carry you much faster than legs. Riding in a car on a freeway, you can travel more than 15 times faster than you can walk.

• Even if you stay in bed all day, you will travel about 1.5 million miles (2.5 million km)! That's how far the Earth moves through space in 24 hours, as it goes around the Sun.

Which is the fastest car?

A British car called *Thrust 2* set the world land speed record in 1983. Using an aircraft jet engine in place of a normal car engine, it reached nearly 634 miles an hour (1,020 km/h).

• The first car to go faster than 60 miles an hour (100 km/h) was battery-powered. It was called *La Jamais Contente*, and it did this nearly 100 years ago, in 1899.

• The world's fastest sailing craft are sailboards. In good winds, they can zip across the water at more than 50 miles an hour (80 km/h).

Spirit of Australia

Which is the fastest boat?

Hydroplanes skim over the water almost as if flying. In 1977, Ken Warby roared to 345 miles an hour (556 km/h) in his jet-powered *Spirit of Australia*.

Thrust 2

SR-71A *Blackbird*

• To carry astronauts to the Moon in the 1960s and 1970s, the Saturn-Apollo rockets had to travel more than 40 times as fast as a jumbo jet. But the top speed of the astronauts' moon buggy was only 10 miles an hour (16 km/h)!

Which is the fastest jet plane?

The official world record speed for jet airplanes was set back in 1976, when a Lockheed SR-71A reached an amazing 2,193 miles an hour (3,530 km/h)! It was nicknamed *Blackbird*.

• One of the quickest ways to travel without an engine is on skis.

Which plane can wiggle its nose?

The superfast passenger jet Concorde can move its nose. With its long slim nose sticking straight out, Concorde can slip through the air at well over double the speed of a jumbo jet. However, when Concorde lands, its nose has to be lowered out of the way. If this isn't done, the pilot can't see the runway!

• Concorde heats up so much in flight that its body stretches — it can get as much as 11 inches (28 cm) longer.

• The world's largest passenger planes, the Boeing 747s, are nicknamed jumbo jets after an elephant. Jumbo was a star attraction at the Barnum and Bailey circus in the 1880s.

Can planes swing their wings?

Yes, some fighter planes have wings that can be moved in and out. This is because wings that stick straight out are the best shape for taking off and landing, and for flying slowly. When wings swing back, they give the plane a smoother shape, which helps it to cut through the air at top speed.

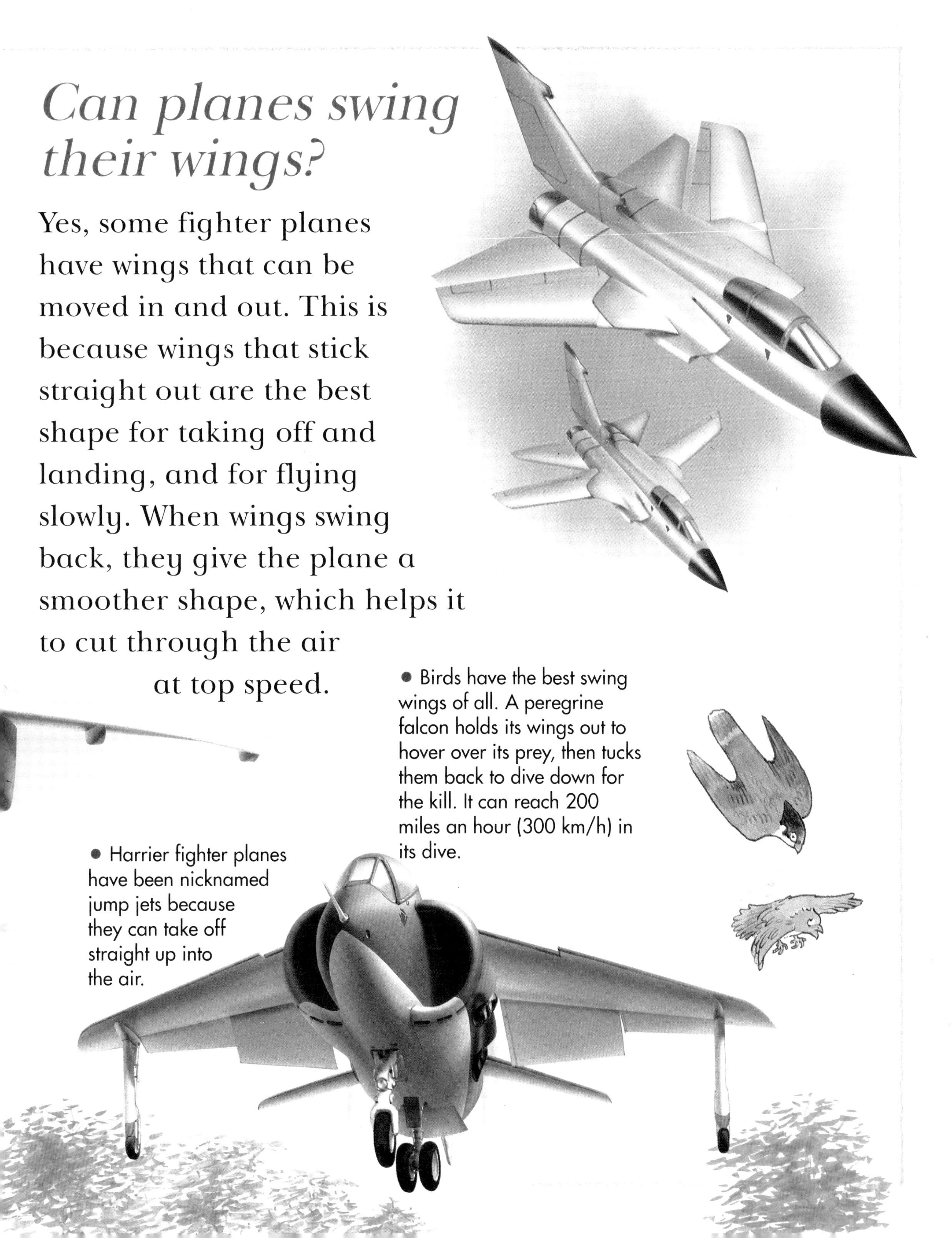

• Birds have the best swing wings of all. A peregrine falcon holds its wings out to hover over its prey, then tucks them back to dive down for the kill. It can reach 200 miles an hour (300 km/h) in its dive.

• Harrier fighter planes have been nicknamed jump jets because they can take off straight up into the air.

Do airships run on air?

Modern airships should really be called gas ships, because they use a gas called helium to help them to fly. Helium helps airships to float because it is lighter than air.

The bag of an airship is called an envelope.

• Fairground balloons are usually filled with helium gas. To see which is lighter, helium or air, try holding a fairground balloon at the same time as a party balloon filled with air.

• The first air letter was carried by a balloon.

• The first-ever balloon passengers were a rooster, a duck, and a sheep! Their 8-minute flight took place over Paris in 1783, more than 200 years ago.

Why do hot-air balloons float?

Balloons float because hot air rises, and hot air rises because it is lighter than cold air. The air inside a hot-air balloon is heated by a burner, which works rather like a camping gas stove.

Why do cars have wheels?

Cars and most other land machines have wheels because wheels make it easier to move. Things slow down when they rub against the ground. Wheels help because they turn easily, and only a small part of them touches the ground.

• Imagine how difficult it would be to move a car if all of it was touching the ground, instead of just its wheels!

• The world's longest car has 26 wheels. It even has room for a tiny swimming pool on board!

• Snow and ice are much more slippery than soil and rock. That's why skis and ice-skates don't need wheels.

Which are the biggest tires?

The world's biggest tires are made for huge dumper trucks, to cushion their heavy loads of rock and earth. The tires are nearly 12 feet (3.6m) high — that's about three times as tall as you are!

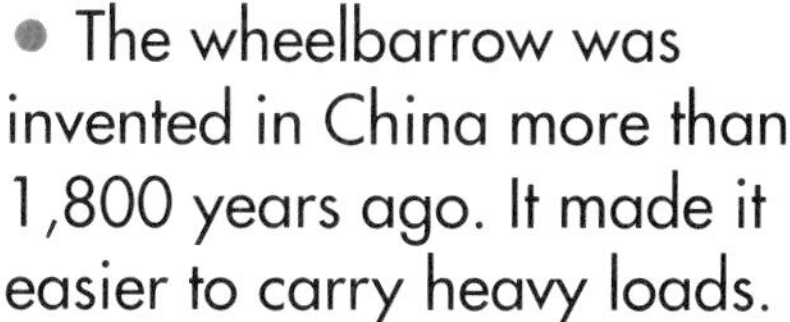

• The wheelbarrow was invented in China more than 1,800 years ago. It made it easier to carry heavy loads.

Which ships have wheels?

River boats called paddle-steamers are driven along by wheels. The wheels have wide boards called paddles. As the wheels turn, the paddles push against the water, moving the boat along.

Why do cars need gasoline?

A car needs gasoline for the same reason that you need food — to give it energy to move. It's hard to tell by looking at it, but gasoline has lots of energy locked up inside it. This energy is set free inside a car engine, so it can be used to turn road wheels.

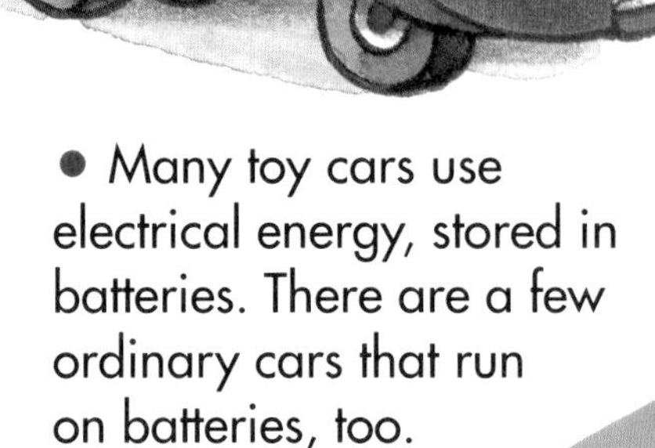

• Many toy cars use electrical energy, stored in batteries. There are a few ordinary cars that run on batteries, too.

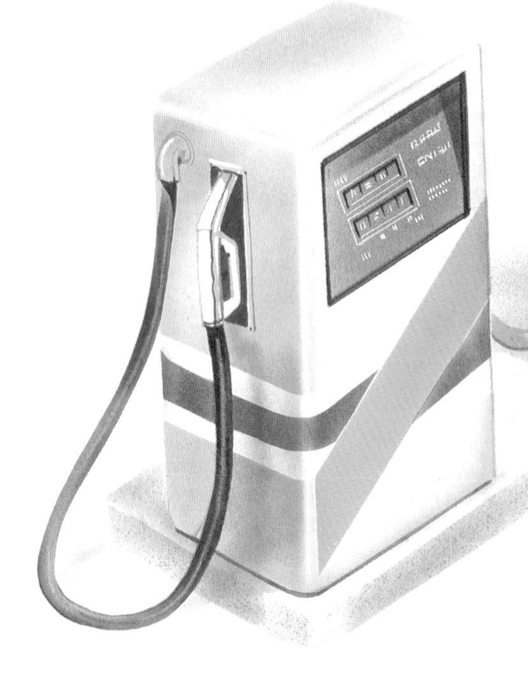

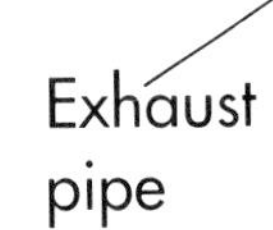

• Gasoline is made from oil, and it has energy because it comes from things that were once living! Oil formed millions of years ago, from the bodies of tiny plants and animals.

• Gasoline is kept in a tank. It is pumped along a pipe to the engine.

• The world's biggest gas station is in Jeddah, Saudi Arabia. It has over 200 pumps!

Pistons

What happens inside car engines?

Gasoline is mixed with air inside a car engine and then set on fire by an electric spark. This makes the air and gasoline explode with a bang. This explosion pushes engine parts called pistons up and down very quickly. The pistons make a rod called the crankshaft spin around. The crankshaft makes other rods spin, and they turn the road wheels.

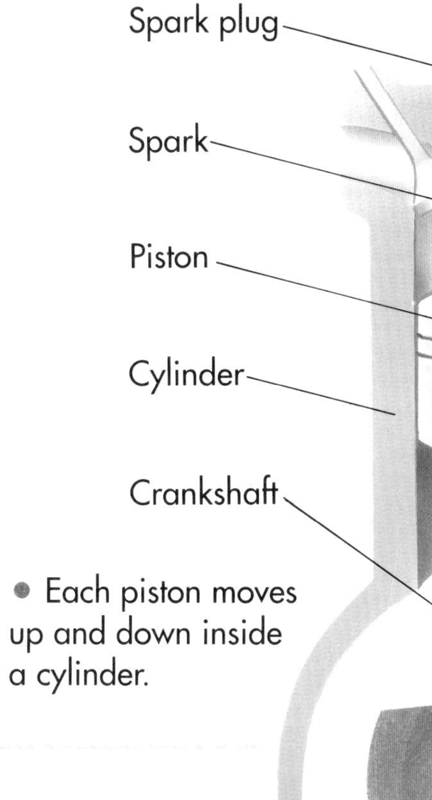

• Each piston moves up and down inside a cylinder.

Do road trains run on rails?

No, road trains run on roads. They are called trains because they are made up of trucks pulling lots of trailers, in the same way that locomotives haul cars.

• Not all trains need drivers. Some city trains are controlled by computers.

• Australian trucks and cars often have strong metal bull-bars fitted in front to cut down damage if they hit large animals such as kangaroos or cattle on outback roads. Another name for them is roo bars ("roo" is short for kangaroo).

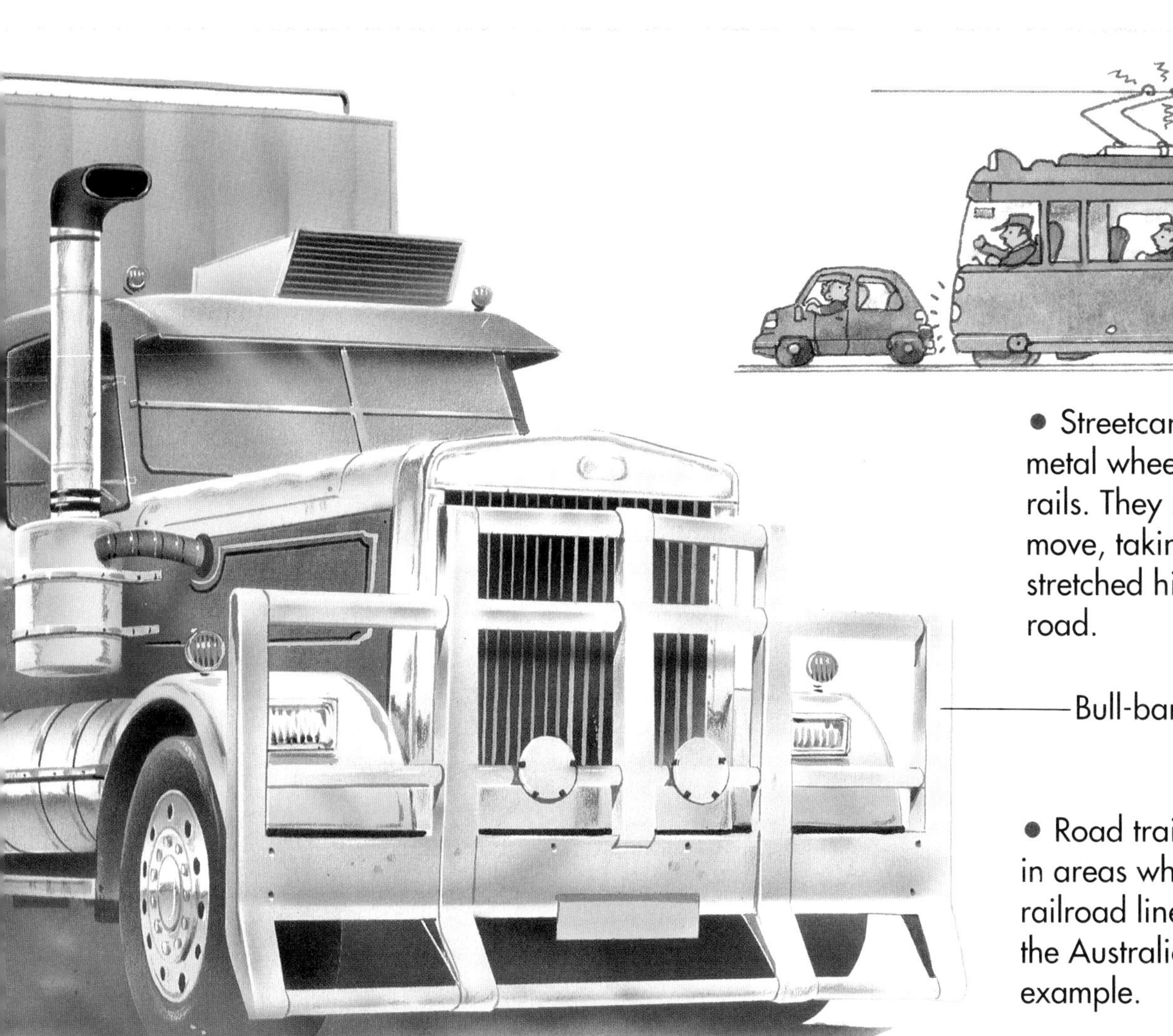

- Streetcars are buses with metal wheels that run on rails. They use electricity to move, taking it from cables stretched high above the road.

- Road trains are often used in areas where there are no railroad lines — in parts of the Australian Outback, for example.

Can trains fly?

Maglevs are a kind of passenger train which float just above a special track. They are lifted and driven by the power of magnets, and they can travel very fast — at over 250 miles an hour (400 km/h)!

Why don't ships sink?

• You push water aside when you get into a bath. That's why you have to be careful not to overfill it!

When things are put into water they make room for themselves by pushing the water aside. Although ships are heavy, they are hollow with high sides. This means they can settle quite low in the water, pushing a lot of it aside. In fact, a ship won't sink unless it is overloaded and becomes heavier than the water it pushes aside.

How do submarines sink?

Submarines sink by making themselves too heavy to float. Water is let into special tanks to add weight. When it's time for a submarine to resurface, the water is pumped out.

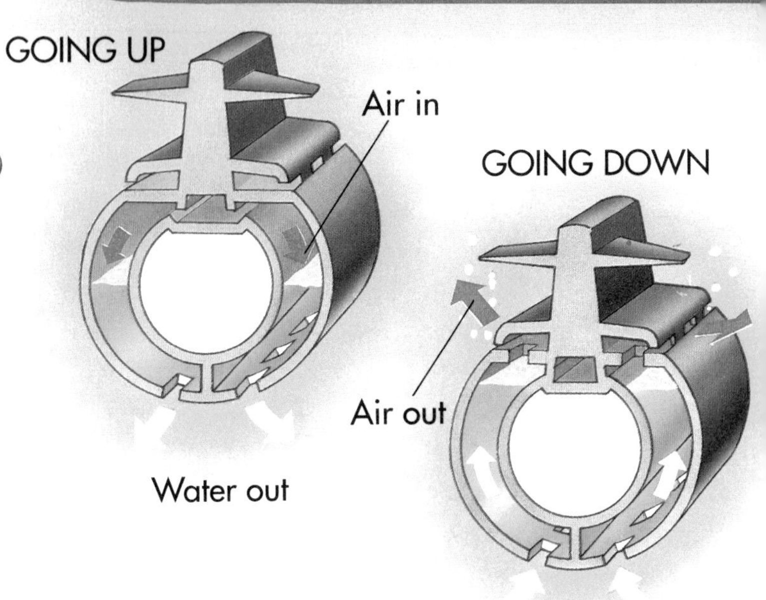

Which ships fly?

Although hovercraft travel across water, they don't float in it like ships. Instead, they hover just above the waves, held up by a cushion of air.

• Hovercraft can travel over land as well as water.

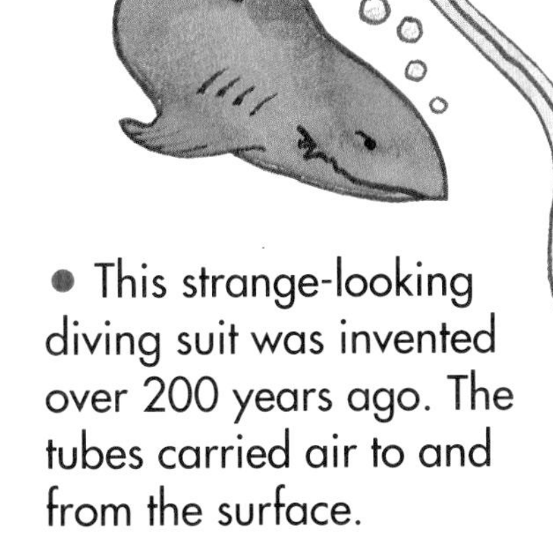

• This strange-looking diving suit was invented over 200 years ago. The tubes carried air to and from the surface.

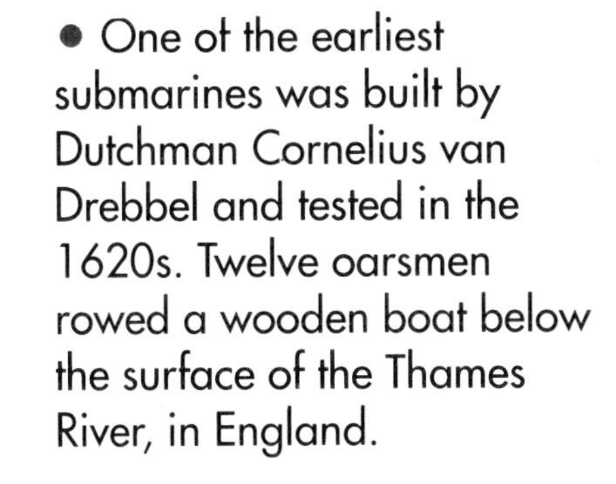

• One of the earliest submarines was built by Dutchman Cornelius van Drebbel and tested in the 1620s. Twelve oarsmen rowed a wooden boat below the surface of the Thames River, in England.

Which plane flies piggyback?

It's not every day that you see a plane riding piggyback, but it does happen. The Shuttle orbiter carries people into space and back again. When it returns to Earth from space it sometimes lands in California, thousands of miles from its takeoff base in Florida. To get back home again, it rides piggyback on a jumbo jet.

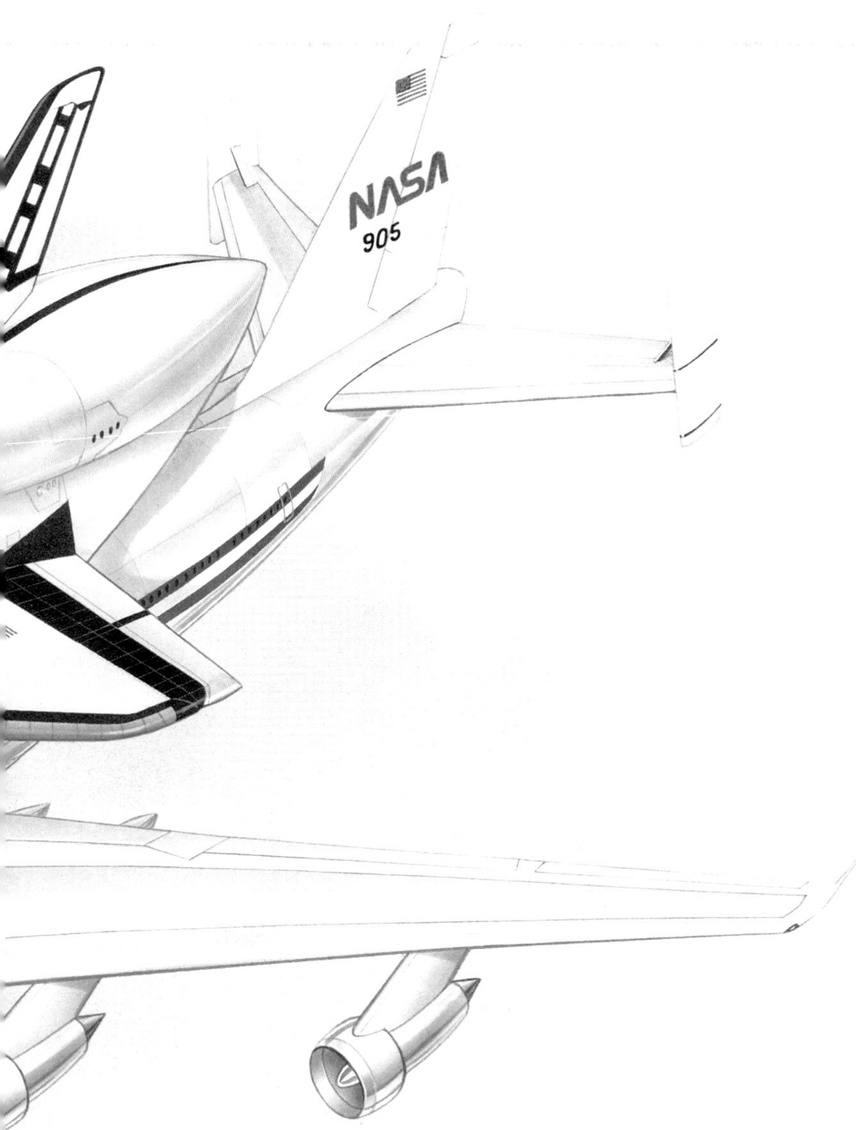

• Ships can ride piggyback, too, on special heavy-lift ships! First, the heavy-lift ship makes itself sink — not completely, but low enough for a smaller ship to float on to its deck. When it rises up again, the smaller ship gets a ride.

1

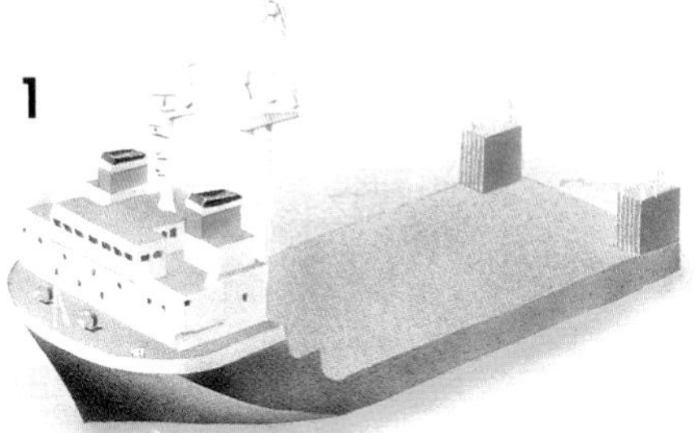

2

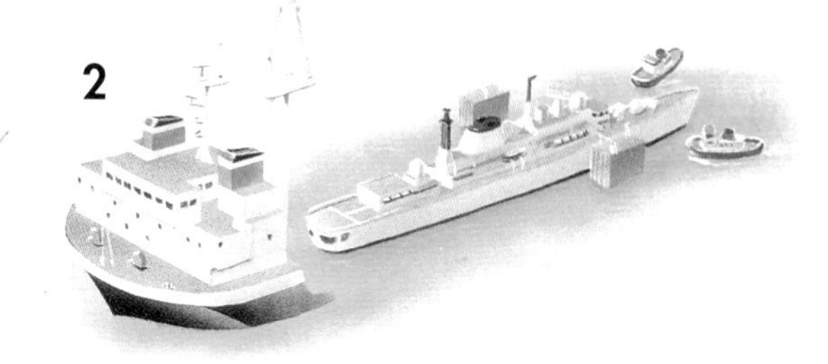

3

When do cars hitch rides?

It's usually people who hitch rides in cars, but sometimes cars themselves get taken for a ride. It happens when new cars are carried on trucks or trains from the factories where they are made, to showrooms where they are sold.

• It may sometimes look as if cars are about to roll off transporters, but don't worry — they're tied firmly in place.

What are houses made from?

Many houses are made from wood or bricks, but they can be built out of almost anything—as long as it's strong and it keeps out the weather. Builders like to use materials they can get hold of easily—bricks or stone, wood, reeds, or mud.

• Bricklayers put mortar between the bricks. Mortar is a mixture of water, sand, and cement, and it glues the bricks together.

• Houses protect us from the heat in summer, and the cold and rain in winter.

• There are about 12,000 bricks in the outside walls of a two-story house.

- Some birds use mud to build their homes, but it's not shaped into little bricks!

- There aren't any bricks in the middle of a forest, but there's plenty of wood for building cabins.

- In the marshes of southern Iraq, in the Middle East, people use bundles of river reeds to build beautiful homes.

- In hot places such as Africa, people often build with mud and straw. The mixture dries hard in the sunshine.

What holds up the ceiling?

The weight of ceilings and floors is carried by strong wooden beams called joists. There are joists hidden away under the floorboards and above the ceiling of every room.

• The roof is held up by thick wooden rafters. Tiles keep out the rain.

• Sometimes uninvited visitors live under the floor, such as the wood-eating grubs of the woodworm beetle.

What's behind the walls?

Among other things, there's usually a lot of air! That's because most brick houses have double outer walls, with a gap between the walls. Pipes and electrical wiring are tucked away in this gap.

• Building a house is teamwork. A plumber lays all the pipes, an electrician does the wiring, and a carpenter puts in the windows, doors, and cupboards.

What's under the floor?

There are pipes under the floor. Some carry clean water around the house. Others take dirty water away. Some aren't for water at all—they carry gas for use in gas stoves, or hot-air ducts for heating the house.

Why do houses need holes?

Most houses start with holes in the ground. The holes are filled with runny concrete, which hardens as it sets. The rest of the house is then built on top of this firm base, called the foundation.

• Many backhoe loaders have a wide front bucket, as well as the digging bucket at the back.

• A backhoe loader can dig a trench as fast as 20 people with spades.

• The biggest earth-scooping buckets can hold five large family cars. They are on huge mining machines called excavators, which are ten times bigger than the average backhoe loader.

• Backhoes also dig holes for swimming pools, garbage dumps, and top secret underground hiding places!

What do backhoe loaders do?

A backhoe loader does much more than dig. Its wide front bucket is great at scooping rubble into a truck. A scissorlike bucket can also be fitted to the front, to grab and lift logs and pipes.

- A huge hammer can be fitted to a backhoe, allowing it to smash up rocks.

Do buildings have roots?

Skyscraper foundations are called piles and they are made of steel or concrete. Piles do the same job for a skyscraper as roots do for a tree. They stop it blowing over in the wind, or sinking into the ground under its own weight.

Which are the world's biggest hammers?

To knock a nail into wood, you use a hammer. To drive a steel pile into the ground, builders use a huge hammer called a pile driver. A crane lifts up the pile driver, then drops it onto the pile with a deafening BANG!

Which are the world's largest corkscrews?

Sometimes, the holes for piles are drilled with an auger—a long tool that works like a giant corkscrew, twisting its way deep down into the ground. A steel rod is put into the hole, and then lots of concrete is poured down around it.

• The piles for some skyscrapers are well over 150 feet deep. That's the same as five houses buried one on top of another!

• Using pile drivers at night is against the law in many towns and cities. They're much too noisy.

Do buildings have a skeleton?

Nowadays, most big buildings have a strong steel framework inside them. This framework does a similar job to the bony skeleton inside your body. It props up the building and stops it from collapsing to the ground.

- Some beams are joined by big nails called rivets. These are punched through holes. Then their ends are flattened to stop them slipping out again.

- Other beams are joined by welding. The ends are heated until they melt and flow together like runny chocolate. When they cool down, the joined ends have hardened together.

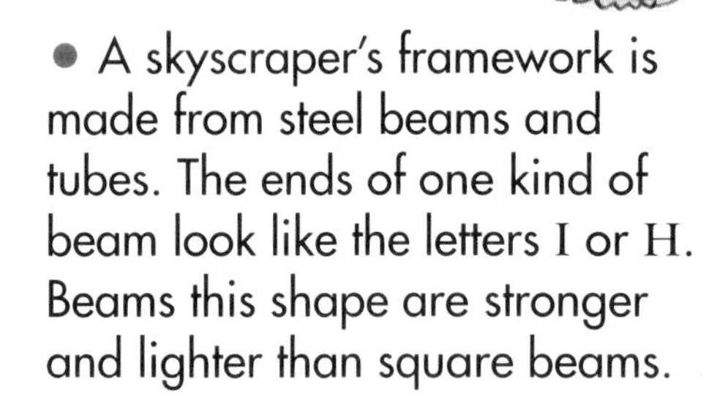

- A skyscraper's framework is made from steel beams and tubes. The ends of one kind of beam look like the letters I or H. Beams this shape are stronger and lighter than square beams.

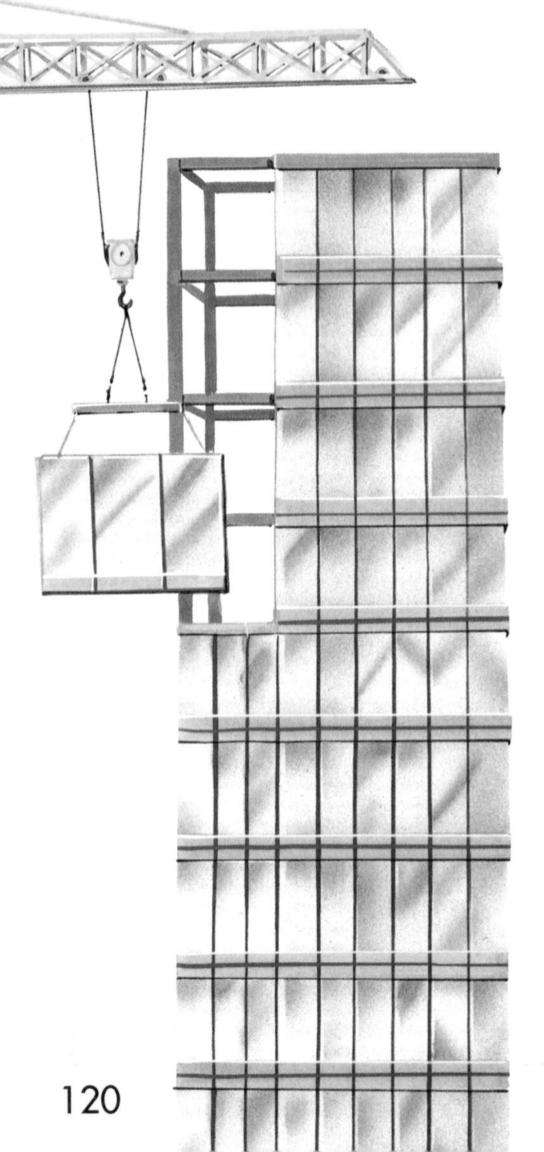

Do buildings have a skin?

The skin of a building is formed by its windows and walls. On modern skyscrapers these are made of glass or plastic panels, and thin concrete or stone sheets. These panels and sheets are called cladding.

Why are some buildings knocked down?

Buildings are knocked down when they are so old or damaged that they're unsafe. Or when someone wants to put a bigger, better building in their place. The quickest way to destroy them is to blow them up with explosives.

• It only takes a few seconds to blow a building up, but it takes a lot longer to work out how to do it safely! Experts decide how much explosive to use, and where to place it.

How do you wreck a building?

You smash it to pieces by swinging a huge metal wrecking ball from a crane! At 10 tons, a big wrecking ball weighs as much as 14 cars, and can do a lot of damage as it smashes into a wall.

- A warning whistle or hooter tells everyone that the building is about to explode!

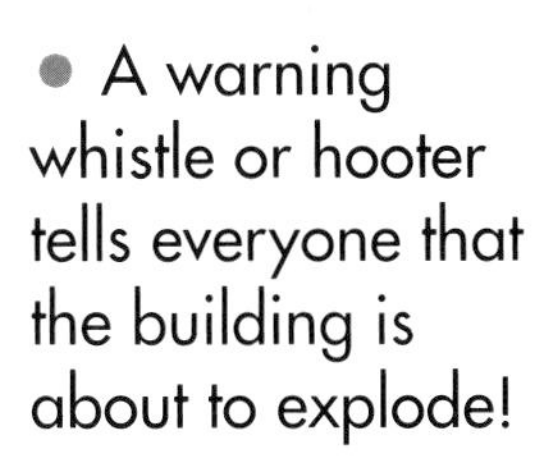

- Canadian karate experts once knocked down a seven-room farmhouse with their bare hands and feet in just over 3 hours.

How do you clean up all the mess?

Bulldozers start by pushing all the rubble into big heaps. Then frontloaders scoop it up and load it into dump trucks. The trucks drive off to a special disposal area and dump their loads. Then they return to the construction site for more.

Which are the world's tallest buildings?

Skyscrapers are the world's tallest buildings—but they've only held the record for 100 years or so. Before then, the world's tallest buildings were the great cathedrals of Europe.

3 The Eiffel Tower, Paris, France, 984 feet high, built in 1887-89.

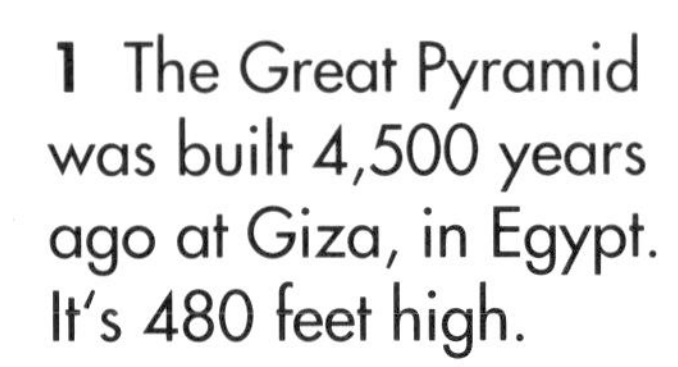

• In some skyscrapers, people live high above the clouds. They have to phone down to find out if it's raining at street level!

1 The Great Pyramid was built 4,500 years ago at Giza, in Egypt. It's 480 feet high.

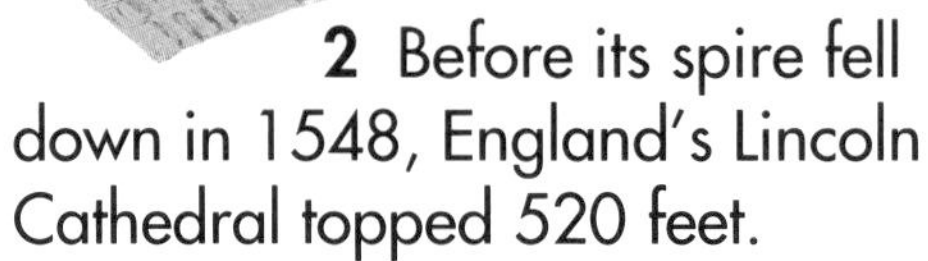

2 Before its spire fell down in 1548, England's Lincoln Cathedral topped 520 feet.

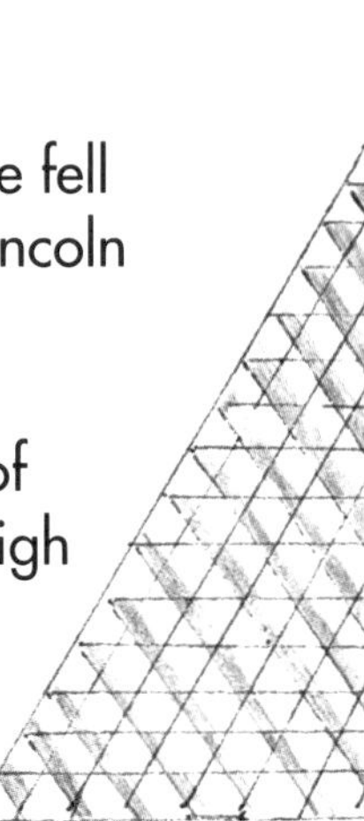

• The world's tallest house of cards was well over 13 feet high —that's probably higher than your bedroom ceiling.

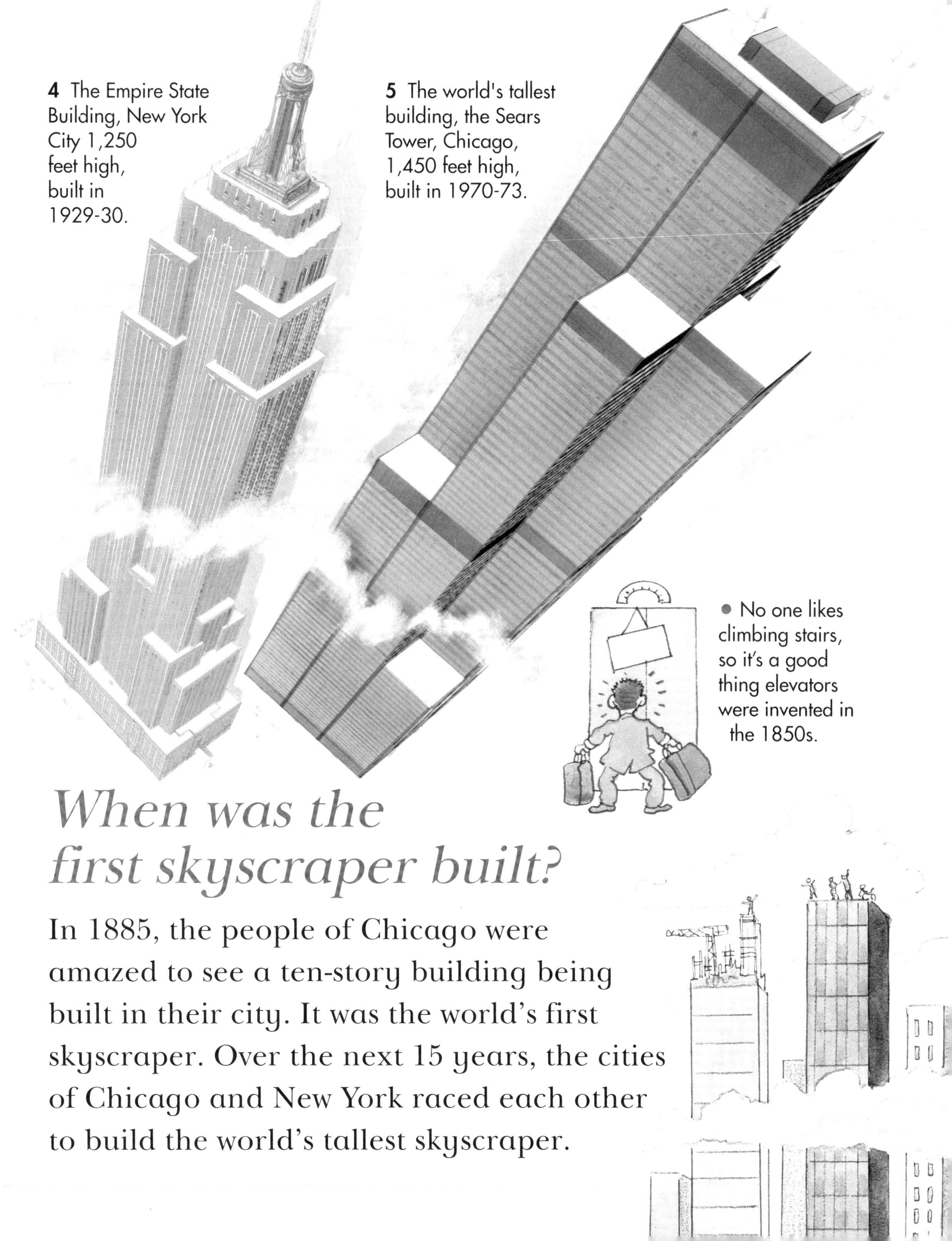

4 The Empire State Building, New York City 1,250 feet high, built in 1929-30.

5 The world's tallest building, the Sears Tower, Chicago, 1,450 feet high, built in 1970-73.

• No one likes climbing stairs, so it's a good thing elevators were invented in the 1850s.

When was the first skyscraper built?

In 1885, the people of Chicago were amazed to see a ten-story building being built in their city. It was the world's first skyscraper. Over the next 15 years, the cities of Chicago and New York raced each other to build the world's tallest skyscraper.

Which roof opens when the sun shines?

The SkyDome sports stadium in Toronto, Canada, has a roof that can open and close. Three gigantic steel panels slide back in good weather to make the stadium open-air. If it starts to rain, the roof closes again—but it takes 20 minutes, so don't forget your umbrella!

• Seafood is so popular in Japan that there's even a fish-shaped restaurant. It's in a large seaport called Kobe.

Which building is inside out?

The outside of the Pompidou Center in Paris is covered in things that are normally hidden away inside. There are elevators, stairs, water pipes, electricity cables—even bathrooms. It's rather like having your lungs, muscles, and veins on the outside of your body!

• One of the buildings at Disney World in Florida looks like a giant golf ball. Its walls are made up of hundreds of metal triangles.

• This is how the SkyDome's roof opens wide.

Why are tunnels round?

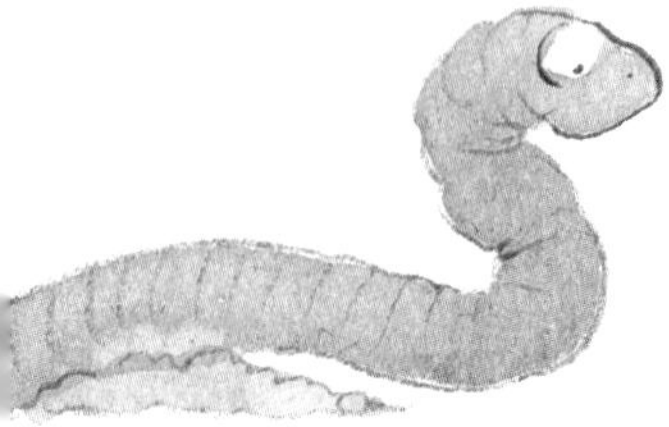

• The Channel Tunnel TBM's cutting head has over 100 cutting rollers and 200 sharp gnashing teeth.

Tunnels are round because drills make round holes! Even tunnels dug with shovels have arched roofs. That's because an arch is a much stronger shape than a square. Big tunnels are carved out by tunnel-boring machines (TBMs, for short). These are like gigantic drills, twisting and grinding their way through the ground.

• The Channel Tunnel between Britain and France is 30 miles long. If all the earth and rock from the tunnel were piled up, it would be nearly twice as tall as the Eiffel Tower.

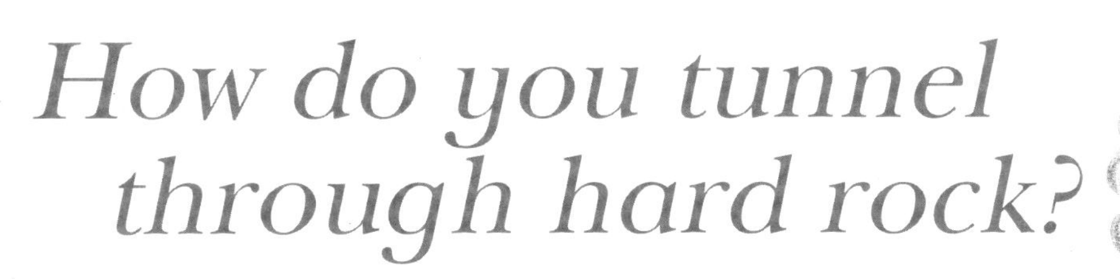

How do you tunnel through hard rock?

Even the most powerful TBM can't cope with really hard rock. Tunnel-builders have to use explosives to blast their way, a little bit at a time.

• Tunnels aren't just for big things like cars and trains. Smaller tunnels carry electricity cables, as well as gas, water, and sewage pipes.

Can a mole dig as fast as a TBM?

A mole can dig five times faster than a TBM, using nothing but its two front paws. It's a lot smaller, though, and so are its tunnels! You can probably guess what the TBM's nickname is—the mole, of course!

How are bridges built?

Like all buildings, bridges start with deep foundation holes. These are filled with metal and concrete, then towers called piers are built on top. The deck is often made from sections, hoisted into place by cranes. Finally, the road or railroad is laid on top of the deck.

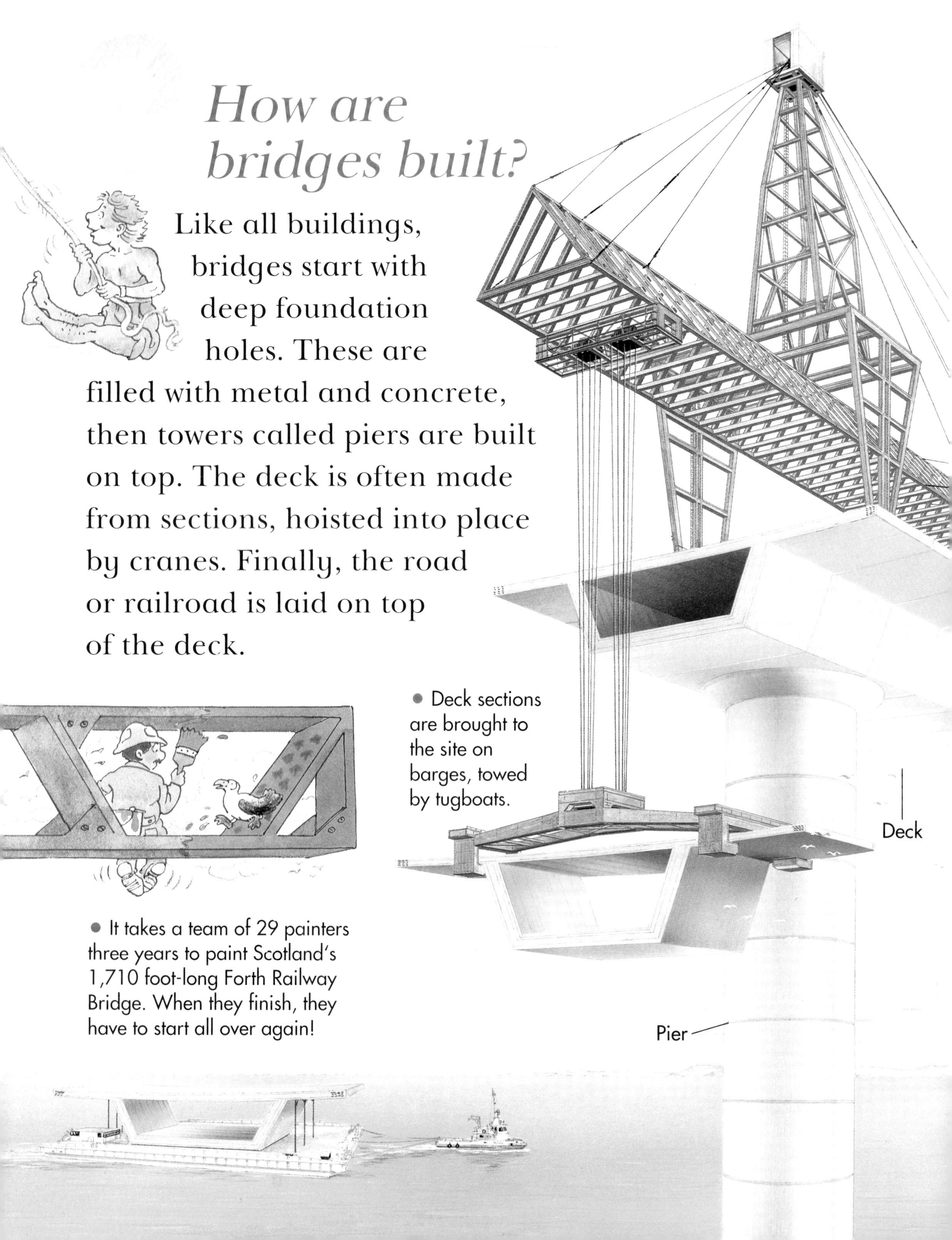

• Deck sections are brought to the site on barges, towed by tugboats.

• It takes a team of 29 painters three years to paint Scotland's 1,710 foot-long Forth Railway Bridge. When they finish, they have to start all over again!

• Soldiers break step when crossing small bridges. If they all marched across in step together, the bridge might bounce. Too much bouncing, and it might break!

• If army ants have to cross gaps, some of them make a living bridge for the others to crawl over.

Do bridges sway in the wind?

Bridges can bend and sway as much as 6 or 10 feet—but don't worry, they're meant to! If bridges were completely rigid, a very strong wind might crack them.

Which bridge can break in two?

London's Tower Bridge carries traffic over the Thames river. The roadway is built in two halves, which can be raised or lowered like drawbridges. When a tall ship sails up the river, each half of the bridge lifts up so that the ship can pass through.

- Bungee-jumpers love the Royal Gorge Bridge in Colorado. At 1,053 feet above the surface of the river, it's the highest bridge in the world.

- Tower Bridge isn't named for its tall towers, but after its neighbor, the Tower of London.

INVENTIONS

Why do people invent things?

Inventors try to solve problems. They think about people's needs and come up with an answer. When an inventor noticed how inconvenient big umbrellas were, he invented a folding one that would fit in a bag.

• From the moment you wake up you're surrounded by inventions. Pillows, light bulbs, and even cornflakes all help to give us a more comfortable life.

Gone to buy some glue!

• Post-it notes were invented by accident when someone made a glue that didn't stick properly. You could stick down a piece of paper, peel it off, and then restick it!

• Some inventions are just for fun. The first Frisbees were empty pie plates belonging to a baker called Joseph Frisbie. When some of his customers tossed the plates to each other in the park, the idea for the Frisbee was born.

• Safety pins were introduced almost 200 years ago but have a much longer history. Their inventor copied the idea from clasps worn by the ancient Egyptians.

Is everything invented?

No it isn't! An invention is something new like a paper clip, which never existed before someone thought of it. But things like coal and rubber weren't invented. They were already in the world and just had to be discovered.

• When people first discovered the milky juice of the rubber tree they used it to make rubber. Later, someone invented rubber tires for cars and bicycles.

Where do inventors get their ideas?

Inventors get ideas for their inventions in lots of different places. Some of them study plants and animals to see how they have solved their problems. Others look at ideas from other places or from the past. Very few ideas come out of the blue.

• Burdock seeds are covered with tiny hooks that stick to things but can be pulled off. An engineer who noticed this used his discovery to make Velcro for fastenings.

Which calendar was carved in stone?

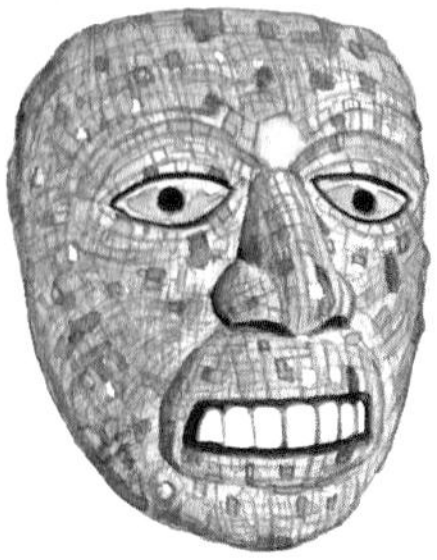

Many thousands of years ago, people called the Aztecs lived in Central America. They made a calendar from a huge stone shaped like the Sun. The face of the Sun god was carved in the middle, and signs for the days were carved all around the edge.

Who invented our calendar?

More than 2,000 years ago a Roman ruler called Julius Caesar invented the calendar we use today. He gave each year 365 days, and arranged them in 12 months. Since then, the calendar has hardly changed.

• The Aztec calendar stone measured nearly 13 feet from side to side—that's far too big to hang on the wall!

What is a leap year?

Every four years we have what we call a leap year. This is a year with 366 days instead of 365. The extra day is added to the end of February. So if your birthday falls on February 29th, it's a very special day indeed.

• A leap year can always be divided by four with none left over. The years 1996, 2000, and 2004 are all leap years.

Why do we need calendars?

Most of us need calendars to help us remember all the things we plan in a year. But they also help us keep track of time. When people are shipwrecked or taken hostage, they find unusual ways to mark the passing days.

Why does my watch tick?

More than 20 tiny wheels are packed neatly inside a windup watch. One part inside the watch goes back and forth to make the ticking sound and turn the wheels. The moving wheels keep time and slowly turn the hands around the watch face.

How did people manage before clocks?

Before there were clocks, people judged the time by looking at the Sun. They got up at sunrise and went to bed when it was dark. They ate lunch when the Sun was high overhead, and ate dinner when it set in the west.

• Sailors traditionally work for four hours at a time. Bells ring every half hour—one after half an hour, two after an hour and so on. When eight bells sound, the shift is over, and the sailors take a well-earned rest.

How does a grandfather keep good time?

A grandfather clock has a long pendulum that swings back and forth in a steady rhythm. With every swing, wheels inside the clock slowly turn, moving the hands around the face. Winding the clock with a key stops it from slowing down.

• Sundials are one of the oldest kinds of clock. Instead of a moving hand they have a shadow, cast by the Sun. As the Earth turns during the day, the "hand" moves around the clock.

How can you split a second?

Today's electronic timers are so accurate that they can split a second into a million parts. In competitive events, athletes are timed to a hundredth of a second—less than the time it takes you to blink.

Which timer was a load of old rope?

About 400 years ago, a ship's speed was measured with a log tied to a knotted rope. The sailors threw the log overboard, and counted how many knots unwound as the ship moved forward. They used an hourglass to time it accurately. Sailors still measure a ship's speed in knots. One knot is just over one mile an hour.

• Musicians use noisy clicking timers called metronomes to help them keep time when they practice.In an Orchestra they have a silent, waving conductor.

How can you cook an egg with sand?

Four minutes is all it takes for the sand inside an egg timer to run from the top to the bottom. And that's just the right time to boil an egg. Sandglasses are simple and accurate and have been used for hundreds of years. Once the timer has finished, you just turn it upside down to start again!

• Speedometers are attached to the wheels of bicycles to measure how fast the bike is going.

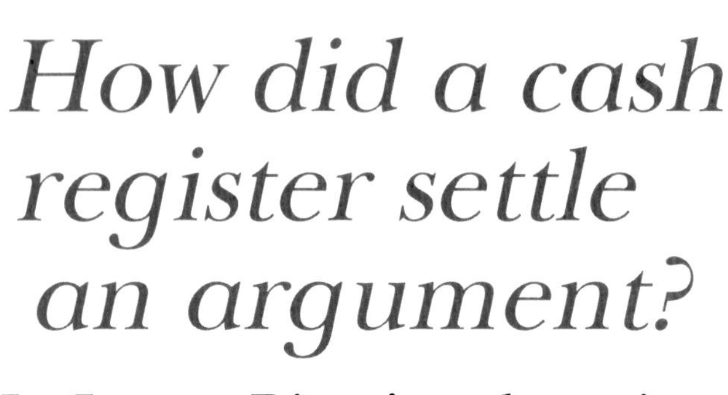

How did a cash register settle an argument?

In James Ritty's saloon in Ohio, customers were always arguing with the staff about how much they had to pay for their drinks. So in 1879 Ritty invented a cash register, which rang up prices, kept a record of how much money had been taken in, and gave Ritty and his staff more peace!

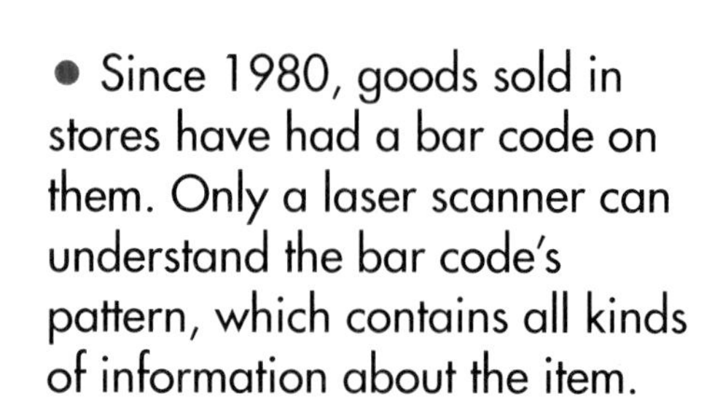

• Since 1980, goods sold in stores have had a bar code on them. Only a laser scanner can understand the bar code's pattern, which contains all kinds of information about the item.

Who used tea as money?

People in Tibet and China once used tea pressed into blocks as money. Before coins were invented, people used to trade things like shells, beads, or grain for the goods they wanted.

• The Chinese first used paper money about 1,200 years ago. They printed some of their bills on the bark of the mulberry tree.

How can a shopping cart make you rich?

The person who invented the world's first supermarket shopping cart became a millionaire. Sylvan Goldman's cart was little more than a chair on wheels with two baskets on top, but it earned him a fortune.

• Inventions don't have to be grand. When Margaret Knight invented flat-bottomed paper bags, she became a wealthy woman. The bags held twice as much shopping!

What did people use before they had refrigerators?

Before about 1920 people kept food cool in wooden cabinets called iceboxes. Huge blocks of ice kept the cabinets cold.

• Coca-Cola didn't start out as a fizzy drink. A pharmacist called John Pemberton invented it as a sweet syrup in 1885. Soda water was added to it later.

Who ate the first cornflakes?

Two brothers, Will and John Kellogg, invented cornflakes by accident when they were trying to make a new type of bread. One day, they overcooked a pan of wheat, rolled the mixture flat, and then watched it dry into flakes. They toasted the flakes and tasted them—delicious!

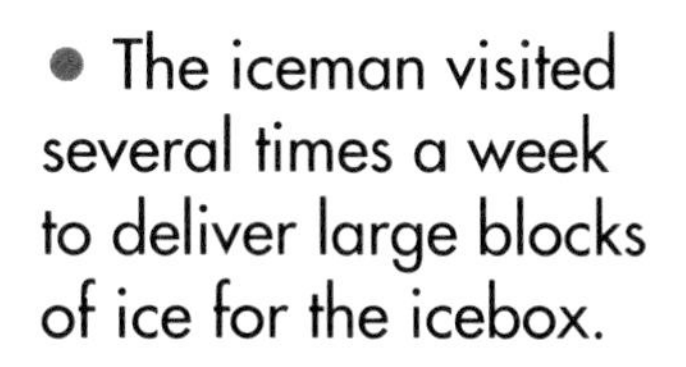

• The iceman visited several times a week to deliver large blocks of ice for the icebox.

• Long ago, people made natural refrigerators by lining caves and holes with a thick layer of snow in winter. These icehouses kept fresh food cool throughout the warm summer months.

• In 1853, a new food was invented. When a diner asked for extra-thin french fries, the chef came up with the first potato chips.

How were drinking straws invented?

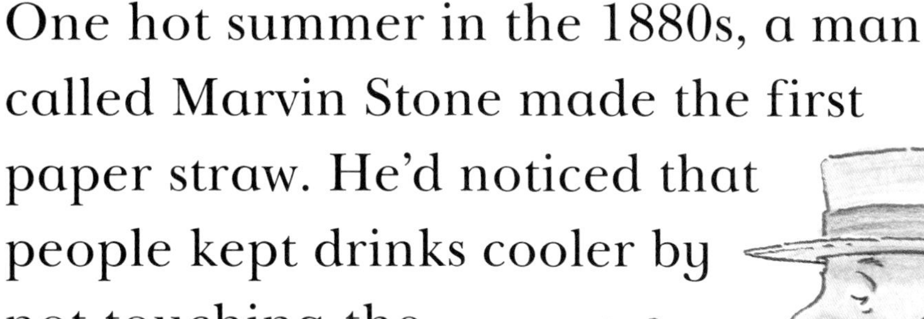

One hot summer in the 1880s, a man called Marvin Stone made the first paper straw. He'd noticed that people kept drinks cooler by not touching the glass and using a hollow grass stalk to suck up the liquid.

How do you make toast without a toaster?

People made toast long before there were electric toasters. They put a piece of bread on the end of a long toasting fork and held it in front of a fire. The bread burned easily, though, and needed very careful watching. The first pop-up toaster was invented about 70 years ago.

• Electric toasters save us from having to keep an eye on the toast—and from burning it, too!

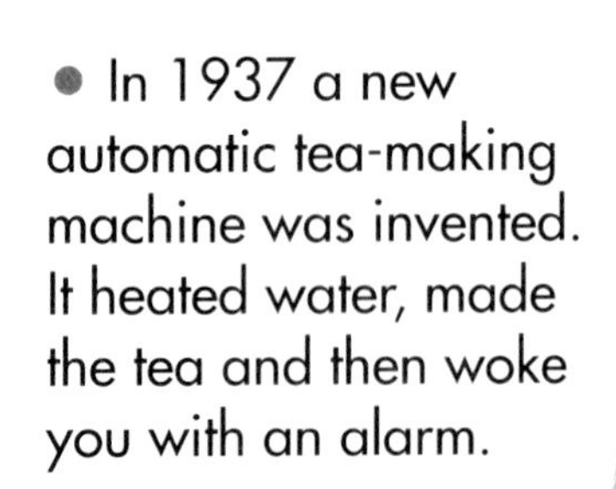

• In 1937 a new automatic tea-making machine was invented. It heated water, made the tea and then woke you with an alarm.

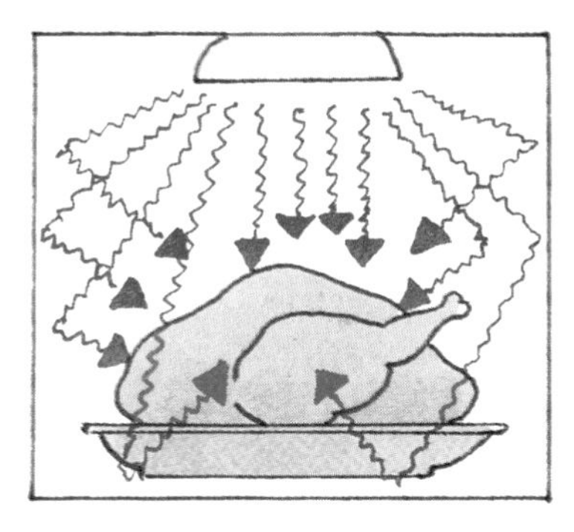

Who invented the microwave oven?

Percy Spencer invented the microwave oven just after World War II. He'd been working on ways of using invisible waves to detect enemy planes. When the waves melted the chocolate bar in his pocket, he realized they'd be useful for cooking too!

• Microwaves are invisible waves of energy. When they're beamed at food, any water in the food starts to shake violently and gets very hot. The heat passes quickly through the food and cooks it all the way through.

• About 100 years ago, only rich people had electricity in their homes. The first electrical gadgets were dangerous things, and servants sometimes risked their lives by using them.

Why don't nonstick frying pans stick?

Nonstick pans don't stick because they are coated with something called Teflon, which is very slippery. Teflon is a kind of plastic and was invented in the late 1930s. It took years for someone to think of sticking the stuff onto pots and pans!

Who first flushed the toilet?

Four hundred years ago Sir John Harrington built a flushing toilet for his godmother, Queen Elizabeth I. In those days few homes had pipes or drains—most people continued to use chamber pots until the late 1800s.

• The problem with this shower from the 1800s was that you had to pump the water yourself—with your foot. No wonder it never really caught on!

• About 100 years ago, flush toilets were highly-prized pieces of furniture. They were often beautifully decorated with fruit, flowers, animals, or shells.

Who first jumped in the tub?

The people of Greece, Rome, and the Indus Valley in Pakistan all enjoyed a bath in ancient times. But as time went by, baths went out of fashion and many people never even washed. They used perfumes to cover up the smell!

• The Chinese used pig's hair to make the first toothbrushes about 500 years ago. Luckily for pigs, nylon brushes came along in the 1930s!

How did horses help keep carpets clean?

The first carpet-cleaning machine was towed by horses! It was parked outside the house because of its smelly gasoline engine. Long pipes stretched through the windows and sucked up all the dirt. It was quite a sight and people often invited their friends around to watch!

Which came first—screws or screwdrivers?

Spiral or twisted nails were used in the 1500s in guns, armor, and clocks. But strangely, you couldn't unscrew a screw for another 300 years—when the handy screwdriver first appeared.

• Today's carpenters use many of the same tools as carpenters long ago.

• Screws weren't made by machine until the 1760s. Before then the thread that runs around the screw had to be filed by hand. That must have been a difficult task!

Who had everything under lock and key?

The ancient Egyptians invented locks. Two wooden bolts fitted together snugly and were held in place by pins arranged in a pattern. The pins could only be freed with a key that had a matching pattern.

• With growing bags you can grow plants anywhere—even if you don't have a yard. These bags of earth first appeared in 1973.

Could a horse mow the lawn?

The first lawn mowers were pulled by horses. The animals had to wear big rubber boots so they didn't leave messy hoof-prints all over the freshly-mowed lawn!

• Lawn mower engines were used on the first go-karts. Today's Grand Prix champions probably all started out driving lawn mowers!

Which new invention was soon on everyone's lips?

In 1915 scientists came up with a small invention that was a huge success. It was a creamy stick of color inside a case that could be twisted up and used on the lips—the very first lipstick.

• Ancient Egyptian women didn't have twist-up lipsticks, but they did color their lips. They used golden clay mixed with juicy tree sap.

Who wore a mouthful of hippo teeth?

Around 2,500 years ago people began to make false teeth from ivory or bone. Hippo bone was popular, but so was ox, cat, and human bone. Unfortunately, all these false teeth soon turned brown and started to rot. They must have tasted disgusting!

• Before lipsticks, lip colors came in a pot. Many of them were waxes and ointments colored with plant dyes such as grape juice.

• A French hairdresser has used a video camera linked to a computer to show his clients what they would look like with different styles—short hair, long hair, or no hair at all!

Why were Band-Aids invented?

Earl Dickson invented Band-Aids for his wife, who often cut herself in the kitchen. He stuck small squares of cloth onto pieces of tape, covering them carefully to stop the glue from drying out. Whenever his wife cut herself, she just grabbed a piece of the tape and stuck it on.

• Before Mr. King Camp Gillette invented safe, modern razors in 1895, men shaved with sharp open razors—and hoped that their hand wouldn't slip!

Who invented raincoats?

• A lot of today's rainwear is made of PVC. It's a plastic-backed material which comes in lots of bright colors.

The first waterproof raincoats were made in 1823 by Charles Macintosh. He made the cloth waterproof by sandwiching a layer of rubber between two lengths of cotton. The coats kept people dry all right, but they weighed a ton and smelled awful when they got wet!

• It rains so much in Scotland that farmers sometimes buy raincoats for their sheep!

Why do zippers have teeth?

The two rows of teeth on a zipper are joined by a slider, which locks them together or pulls them apart. Zippers were invented in the 1890s and were a great improvement on tiny buttons and hooks.

• The first jeans were made by Levi Strauss for gold miners in San Francisco. He made them in a hard-wearing blue cloth that was used to make tents. These days it's better known as denim.

Can clothes keep you feeling fit?

Some clothes can do amazing things. You can even buy panty hose full of health-giving vitamins, which are usually found in fresh fruit and vegetables!

• When Thomas Hancock invented elastic in 1820, he thought it would be useful along the top of pockets to stop thieves. It was someone else who realized it would be just right for holding up people's underwear!

Who scored points in a basket?

The very first basketball players used two old peach baskets as nets. Basketball was invented about 100 years ago by coach James Naismith, who was looking for an exciting game to play indoors on cold winter nights.

Why are sneakers so springy?

Sneakers have springy soles made of rubber and little pockets of air. Each time you take a step, the rubber gets squashed down, but quickly springs back to its original size. All this squashing and springing makes your feet bounce off the ground and helps you to run a little bit faster.

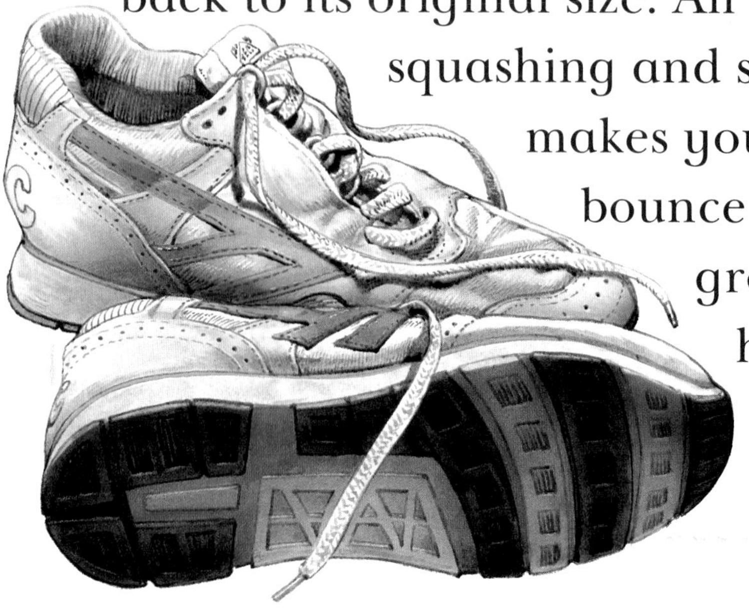

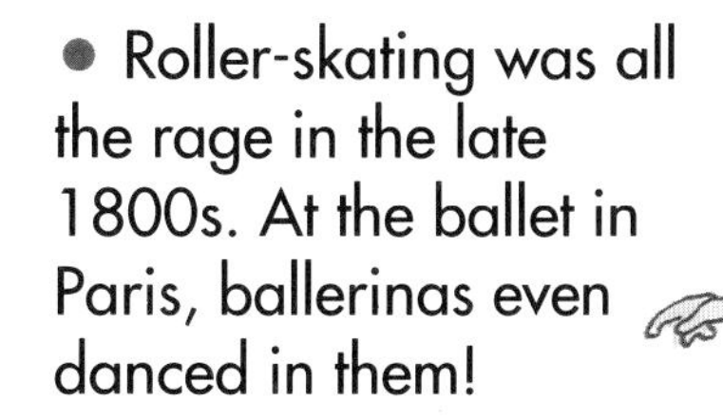

• Roller-skating was all the rage in the late 1800s. At the ballet in Paris, ballerinas even danced in them!

• Early basketball players had to climb a ladder to get the ball back after a basket. Things are easier today—now the nets have a hole in the bottom.

How did people ice-skate in summer?

Before there were ice rinks, people could only ice-skate outdoors in the winter. Then someone came up with the idea of making a "ground" skate that people could enjoy in the summer, too. Instead of a blade, they put wheels on the sole and abracadabra—the roller skate had arrived!

• Jet-skis first went on sale in Japan in 1979. Jet-skiers have to steer well clear of swimmers. The very latest models can zoom along at speeds of 65 mph.

Why are bears called teddies?

Teddy bears are named after President Theodore Roosevelt, who was called Teddy for short. Once, on a hunting trip, he came across a bear cub and refused to shoot it. A candy store owner who read the story in the paper decided to give up his store and make toy bears. He called them teddies, after the president.

• The construction toys Lego and Erector were both invented to encourage children to build things, not destroy them! You can use them to make all sorts of inventions!

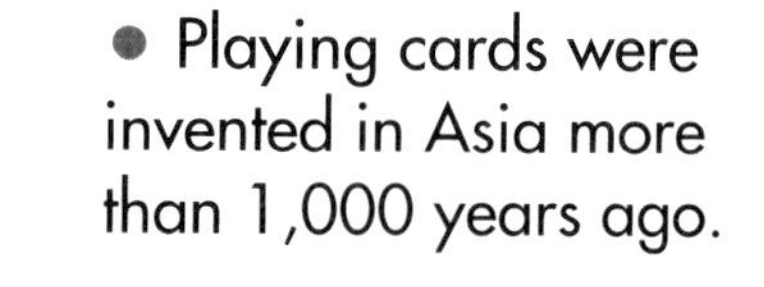

• Playing cards were invented in Asia more than 1,000 years ago.

Which toy is 6,000 years old?

Dolls are probably the oldest toys of all. Roman children played with dolls made of rags. Dolls have been made from all kinds of materials—wood, wax, paper, china, and plastic.

• Barbie went on sale in 1959. She was the first doll ever to have a grown-up's body.

When did home computer games appear?

The first home computer games appeared in 1974. Compared to today's games, they weren't very exciting. There were no life-and-death battles in outer space—you hit a ball back and forth with a bat!

What were the first cars like?

The first cars were steam engines on wheels—noisy, smoky machines that scared other road-users! But these steam cars soon became quicker and easier to drive. They were used for nearly 30 years, until they were replaced by faster cars with gasoline engines.

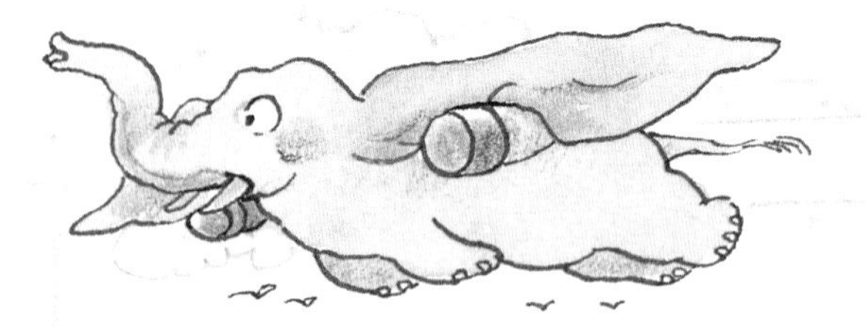

• In the 1930s, planes carried 20 passengers at the most. By the 1970s, the new jumbo jets could seat up to 500! Soon, new super-jumbos will carry as many as 850 people!

How do you ride on air?

People ride on air every time they travel on a hovercraft. The hovercraft was invented by Christopher Cockerell in 1959. He discovered that trapping a cushion of air beneath a boat lifts it up above the waves, allowing it to travel much faster.

• The high-wheeler bicycle was invented in the 1860s. It had two wheels—one very large and one very small.

• Eveyone knows about seat belts for people to wear, but did you know that cats and dogs can wear them too? So buckle up, Rover and Felix!

Which bikes have sails?

• The first cars weren't allowed to go faster than 2 mph. And someone had to walk in front with a flag to warn other road-users!

The fastest superbikes have solid wheels and flat frames that work in the same way as a sail. As the bike zooms along, its wheels and frame catch the wind, which helps to push the bike forward—just as a sail does on a boat. But most of the power still comes from turning the pedals!

Who cycled over the sea?

In June 1979, American Bryan Allen pedaled a special plane called the *Gossamer Albatross* across the Channel, from England to France, in just under 2 hours and 50 minutes.

Nine years later, Kanellos Kanellopoulos of Greece pedaled his *Daedalus 88* over the sea between the islands of Crete and Santorini.

Can bikes climb mountains?

Machines called mountain bikes are specially designed for rough stony ground. Their frames are extra-strong so they can stand up to rattling over bumps, while their knobbly tires grip well even in slippery sand or mud.

• It's not easy to balance on a unicycle — it only has one wheel!

• When the first bicycles were invented, about 200 years ago, they didn't have any pedals! People rolled them along by pushing against the ground with their feet.

How many people can ride on one bike?

Although most bikes are designed for one rider, special bikes are sometimes built to take more. The world's longest bike was built in Belgium. It had seats and pedals for 35 people, but it was very difficult for them all to balance and cycle at once!

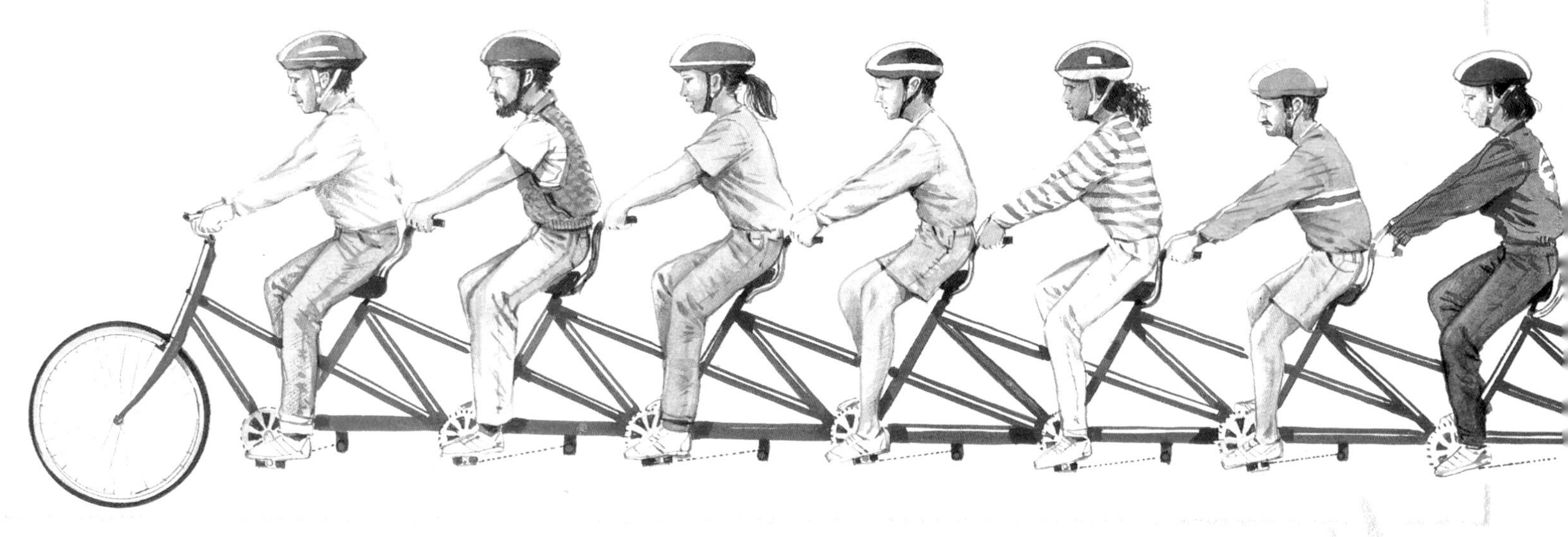

How can you fit 1,000 books in your pocket?

There's room for around 1,000 storybooks on a CD-ROM—a small compact disc that's as thin as your fingernail and can fit in a pocket. Words, pictures, and sounds can all be stored on CD-ROMs, but they only work with a computer, so you can't read one on the bus—yet!

• The Egyptians were one of the first peoples to write with ink. They made it by mixing black soot with sticky tree sap.

• Just like dinosaurs, the typewriter will soon be extinct. It was a new invention in 1873 but has now been replaced by computers and word processors.

• Felt-tip pens went on sale in Japan in 1962. Their inventor hoped that the pen's soft tip would make people's handwriting more graceful—like the brushstrokes in Japanese writing.

• Today's pocket calculators can carry out calculations much quicker than you can move your fingers. They are as powerful as the huge computers of the 1960s.

Which computer was as big as a bus?

The first computer was about as long as four buses and was called Colossus. It was built in Britain and was switched on in 1943. Very few people knew about it at the time, because one of its first jobs was to crack secret codes during World War II.

Who was Mr. Biro?

Ladislao Biro invented a ballpoint pen in 1938. It contained a tube of long-lasting, quick-drying ink, which rolled evenly onto the paper thanks to a tiny ball at the tip. Biro called his pen a ballpoint, but in many countries ballpoints are still called biros!

Who took hours to take a photo?

• In the late 1800s, it took so long to take a photo that sitters needed a backrest to help them sit still!

A Frenchman called Joseph Niépce took the first photograph in 1826. He had to wait eight hours before the picture was captured on a thin metal plate coated with a sort of tar. The photo was of the view from his window.

• Niépce would have found it hard to believe, but today's Polaroid cameras can produce a picture in seconds!

When could you watch pink TV?

The first TV had an odd picture —bright pink and very fuzzy! But its inventor, John Logie Baird, had used very odd equipment to build it, including a bicycle light and a knitting needle!

• The world's smallest radio is about the size of a pea!

Who invented the personal stereo?

A Walkman is a personal cassette player with headphones that is light enough to carry around. It was invented in 1979 by a Japanese electrical company called Sony.

• The first telephone service started in 1878, in New Haven, Connecticut. Only 20 people had phones, so they could only call each other!

Why does the telephone ring?

The telephone rings to let you know that someone wants to speak to you! So if your friend dials your number, your phone rings. When you answer, an electric current carries your voice along the line and your friend hears you loud and clear.

- Today, most telephone exchanges connect calls automatically with computers.

- Telephone calls used to be connected by hand. An operator asked which telephone number you wanted and plugged in the correct wire.

How can glass link the world?

Optical fibers are hair-thin strands of glass, twisted into cable. They have been laid under all the oceans and act as highways for anything from phone calls to TV programs. Information travels along them at the speed of light.

• Telephones come in all shapes and sizes, from tiny mobiles to cartoon characters. But they all have two main parts—the transmitter you talk into and the receiver through which you hear.

Are phone lines just for voices?

Voices aren't the only things that travel along a phone line. With a videophone, you can see a picture of who's telephoning as well. With a fax, you can send letters, photos, and drawings. And computers use phone lines to communicate with one another, too!

• There are more than 100 million telephones in the United States. In Washington, D.C., there are more phones than people!

Can a robot play the piano?

A clever Japanese robot called WABOT-2 can whizz its fingers over a keyboard much faster than a human can. It can either read new music, or choose a song it has played before and stored in its memory. The cleverest thing about WABOT-2 is its sensitive fingers. It can play gently or furiously.

• WABOT-2's head is like a camcorder. As the robot reads music, the camera "films" what it sees and stores it in its memory to play again.

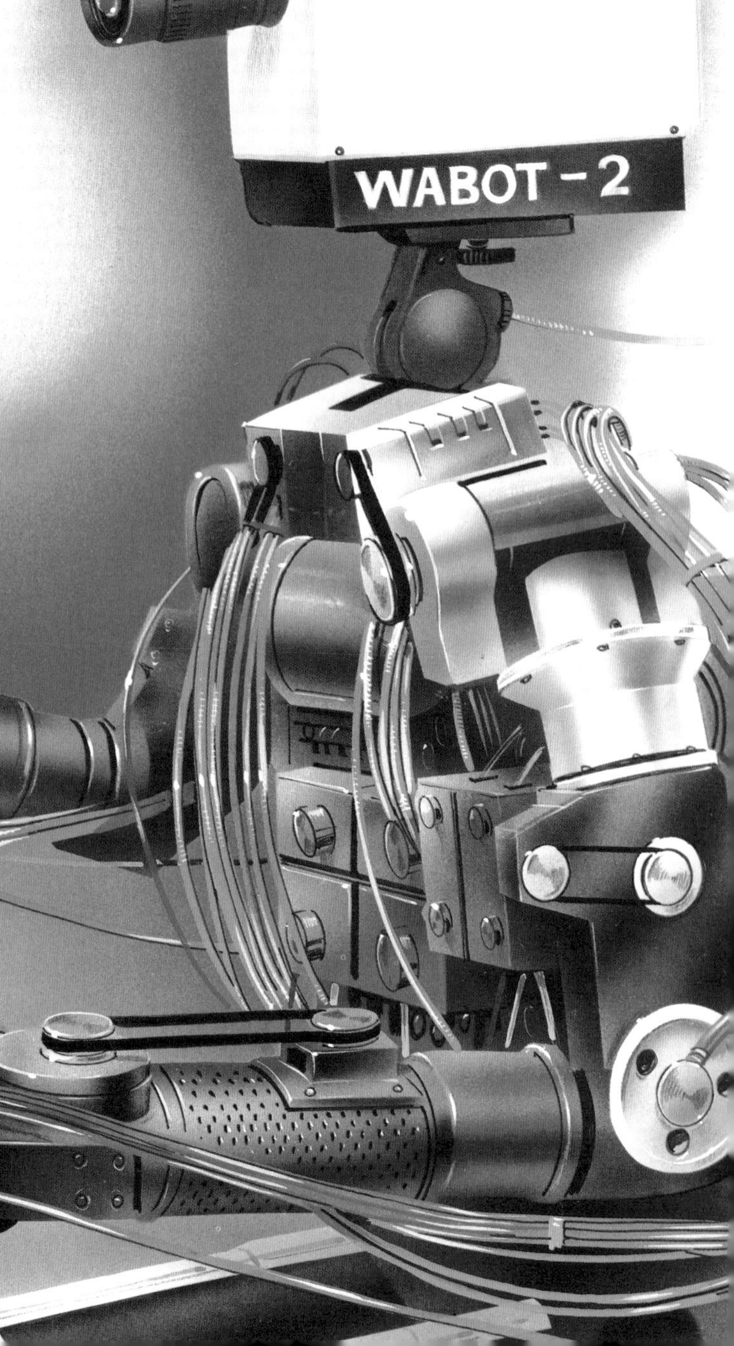

Where do people mix music?

In a recording studio, the voices and instruments are recorded separately. The producer mixes the parts together on a machine called a mixing desk. He or she checks the sounds are balanced and every part can be heard clearly.

• Drum machines make the sound of all kinds of drums—but they're only as big as a candy box. Some of them have pads to tap out the rhythm on.

• You can record any sound you like on a sampler—even a dog's bark. You put the sounds you've sampled into tunes as if they were musical notes.

Can you be an entire orchestra?

Synthesizers are machines that can make the sound of every instrument in the orchestra. One minute they sound like a flute, the next they sound like a violin. They'll even play a simple drum pattern to give your music a beat.

How can you fight a hungry dinosaur?

When you put on a virtual reality helmet, you enter an imaginary world. You could be fighting a man-eating dinosaur or visiting aliens in space. Everything inside the helmet looks and sounds real but is actually created by a computer.

• As you press buttons in the special data-glove, the computer changes the pictures you see and the sounds you hear.

• Anyone can be an inventor! What would you like to invent?

HISTORY

How many dinosaurs were there?

There were lots of different dinosaurs. Scientists have already named about 300 kinds, and new ones are being found all the time. Some dinosaurs were big, others were tiny. Some were fierce meat-eaters, others were gentle vegetarians that browsed on plants.

• Dinosaurs were reptiles. Today's reptiles include lizards, crocodiles, tortoises, and snakes.

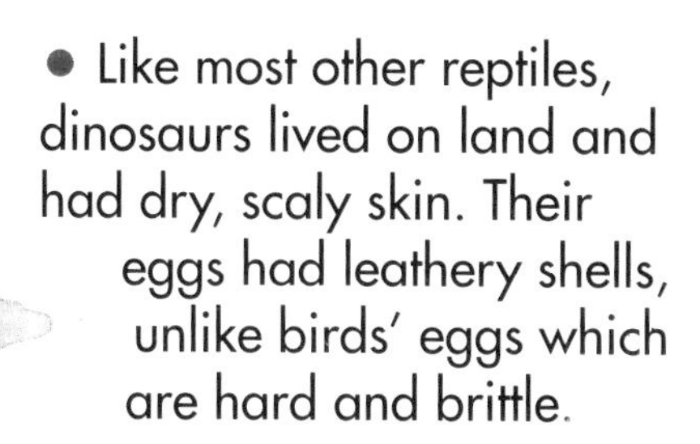

• Like most other reptiles, dinosaurs lived on land and had dry, scaly skin. Their eggs had leathery shells, unlike birds' eggs which are hard and brittle.

How long ago did dinosaurs live?

Dinosaurs lived MILLIONS and MILLIONS of years ago. The first ones appeared about 230 million years ago, and the last ones we know about died out over 65 million years ago. Compared to this, human history is just a hiccup — we've only been around for the last 2 million years.

• Dinosaurs ruled the Earth for a mind-boggling 165 million years!

Kentrosaurus (plants)

How are dinosaur fossils found?

Dinosaur fossils are usually buried inside rock, so they have to be dug out. People sometimes stumble across them by accident, but most fossils are found by scientists who go looking in likely places. This is easier than it sounds, because only some kinds of rock have dinosaur fossils in them.

• One of the first jobs is to make a map of the digging area. Then, each time a fossil is found, it can be marked on the map.

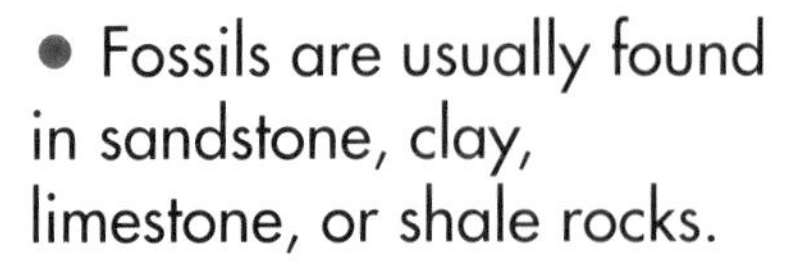

• Fossils are usually found in sandstone, clay, limestone, or shale rocks.

• It may take weeks, months, or even years to dig out a whole skeleton.

• Dinosaurs are sometimes named after the person who found them.

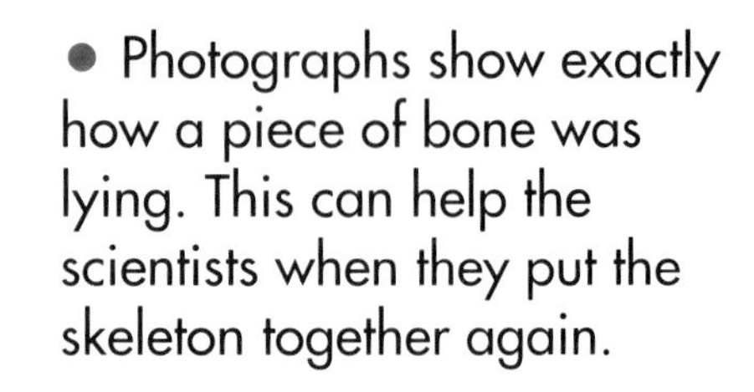

• Photographs show exactly how a piece of bone was lying. This can help the scientists when they put the skeleton together again.

- The finds often have to be carried away by truck over rough bumpy ground.

- Covering a fossil in a thick layer of hard plaster helps to keep it safe from knocks. It's just like putting a plaster cast around a broken leg.

- Dinosaur digs are often in wild places, far from any town or road. The team have to live in tents or trailers.

Where are dinosaurs found?

Dinosaurs lived all over the Earth. Their fossils have been found in places as far apart as the United States and China, England and Australia, even in Antarctica!

What happened to the dinosaurs?

Something very strange happened 65 million years ago. All the dinosaurs vanished, together with all the flying reptiles and most of the sea reptiles. No one knows for sure what happened to them.

• Many scientists think giant rocks from outer space smashed into the Earth, throwing up great clouds of dust which blotted out the Sun. This changed the weather and killed off most plants. First the plant-eating dinosaurs died of cold and hunger, then the meat-eaters.

• Perhaps the dinosaurs were poisoned by new kinds of plants

• A few people believe that sea reptiles like Elasmosaurus didn't die out, and that families of them now live in big lakes like Scotland's Loch Ness!

• Archaeopteryx looked like a dinosaur with feathers, but it wasn't. It lived 140 million years ago, and it is the oldest bird we know about. It was a very strange bird, though, because it had a tail, clawed fingers and teeth, just like a dinosaur.

Are there any dinosaurs around today?

Although there aren't any true dinosaurs alive today, we do have some of their relatives. Scientists think that birds developed from dinosaurs, because their skeletons are so similar. So look carefully the next time you see a bird nesting in a tree or hopping across the grass!

Why do we call Egyptians ancient?

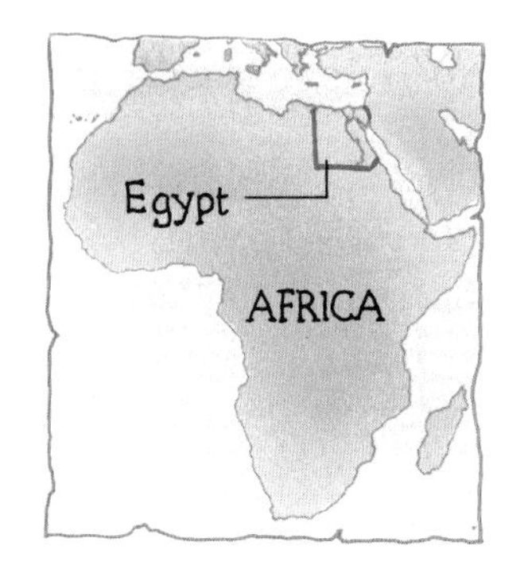

We call the Egyptians ancient because they lived such a long time ago—not because they all reached a ripe old age! The first Egyptians were farmers around 8,000 years ago. Within a few thousand years, Egypt had become one of the most powerful countries in the world.

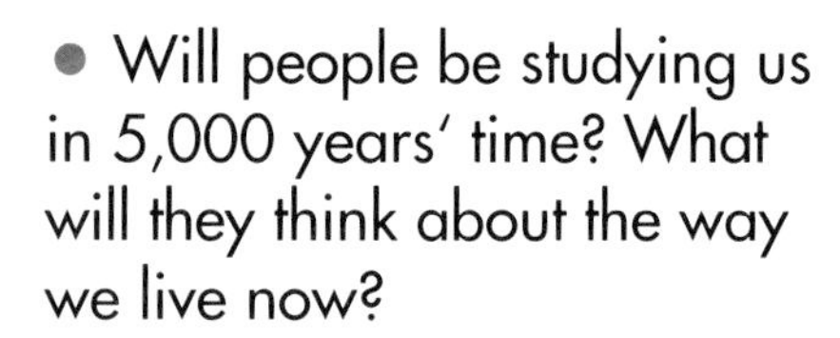

• Will people be studying us in 5,000 years' time? What will they think about the way we live now?

• The Egyptians usually built tombs for dead kings on the river's western bank, where the Sun sets. They believed that their kings went to meet the Sun god when they died.

• Egypt is mostly sandy desert, where nothing grows. The ancient Egyptians settled on the banks of the Nile River, where there was plenty of water for themselves and their crops.

• The ancient Egyptians didn't know about distant parts of the world. But they did explore parts of Asia and Africa. And their merchants bought wood, gold, ivory, spices, and even apes from nearby countries.

Why were the Egyptians great?

The Egyptians were so good at farming that they became very rich. They built fantastic temples for their gods, and huge pointed tombs called pyramids where they buried their kings. They had armies and ships and courts of law. Their priests studied the stars and their craftspeople made beautiful things from gold and silver.

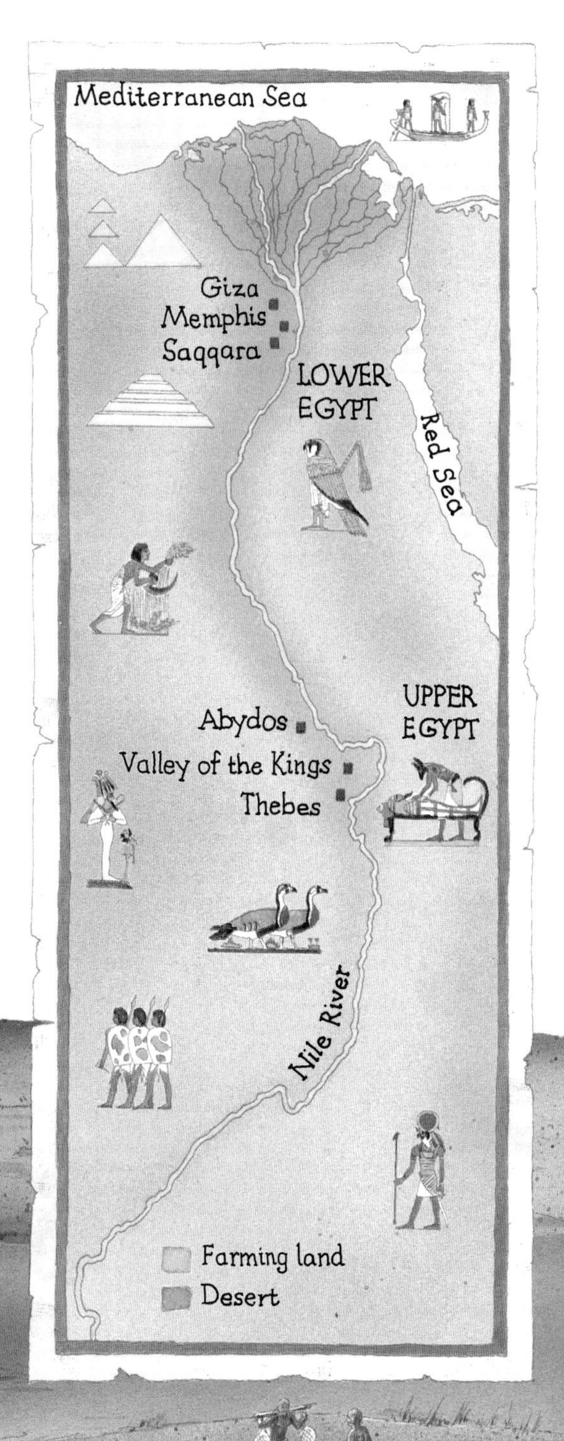

Who ruled Egypt?

The king of Egypt was called the pharaoh. The Egyptians believed that their Sun god Ra was the first king of Egypt, and that all the pharaohs after him were his relatives. This made the pharaoh very holy — and very powerful! The people thought he was a god on Earth.

• The pharaoh's advisors were called the Honored Ones. There were all sorts of royal officials, too, with fancy names like the Director of Royal Dress and the Keeper of the Royal Wigs.

Could a woman be pharaoh?

Although very few women ruled Egypt, there was a famous pharaoh called Hatshepsut. When her six-year-old nephew came to the throne, Hatshepsut was asked to rule Egypt for him — just until he was a little bit older. But Hatshepsut liked ruling so much that she wouldn't let her nephew take over. He didn't get the chance to rule until he was 30 years old!

• When she was pharaoh, Hatshepsut had to wear the badges of royalty. These included a false beard, made of real hair.

How would you know if you met a pharaoh?

He would be wearing a crown, of course! In fact, pharaohs sometimes wore two crowns at the same time—a white one for Upper Egypt, which was the name for the south of the country, and a red one for Lower Egypt, which was the north.

Why did the Egyptians bury their mummies?

A mummy is a dead body which has been dried out so it lasts for thousands of years. The Egyptians believed that the dead traveled to another world, where they needed their bodies. And they didn't want any bits missing!

• Egyptian families had their nearest and dearest mummified, but it was an expensive business. Only the rich could afford a really good send-off.

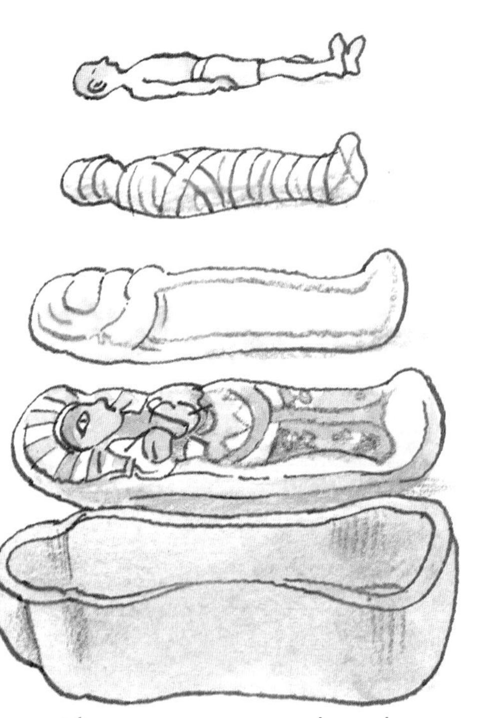

• The mummy was placed inside a series of wooden coffins. These were put in a big stone case called a sarcophagus.

• Monkeys, crocodiles, cats, and other sacred animals were often mummified, too!

Why were mummies brainless?

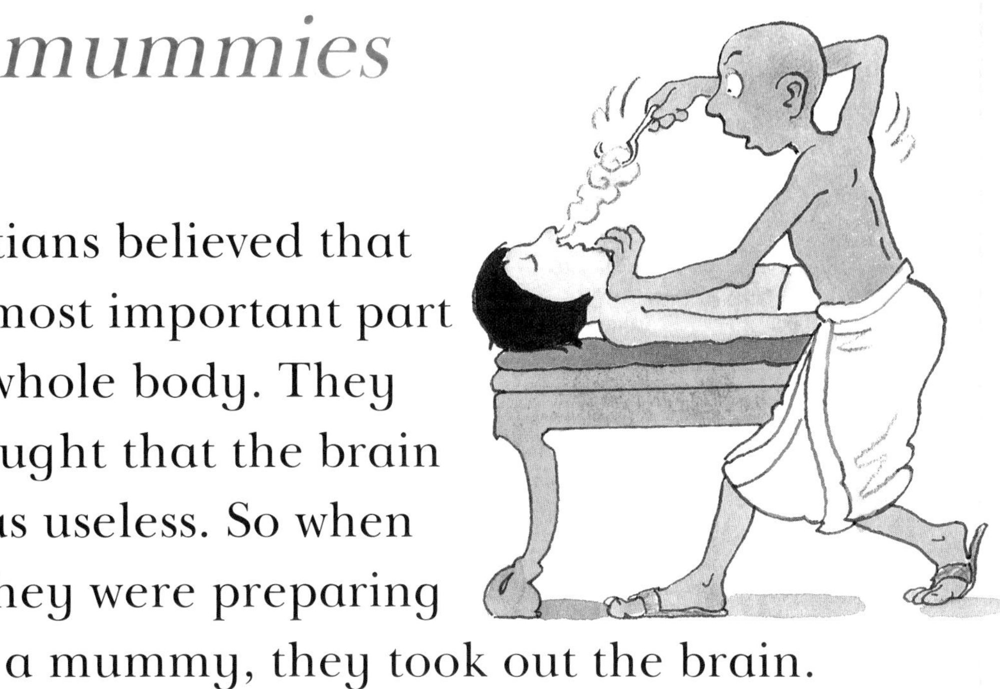

The ancient Egyptians believed that the heart was the most important part of the whole body. They thought that the brain was useless. So when they were preparing a mummy, they took out the brain.

Why were mummies wrapped in bandages?

Wrapping the dead body helped to keep its shape. After the insides were removed, the body was dried out for 40 days in a salty substance called natron. Then it was washed, rubbed with ointments, and bandaged.

Why were the pyramids built?

The pyramids were huge tombs for dead pharaohs and other very important people. No one knows exactly why the pyramids were shaped this way. Some people think they were built to point toward the Sun and stars, so that the dead person's spirit could fly to heaven like a rocket.

• The Great Pyramid at Giza was built more than 4,500 years ago. This is what it looks like today.

• Pharaohs were buried with all their finest clothes and jewelry, so tombs were given sneaky traps to catch out robbers.

• There are other, smaller pyramids at Giza, and more than 80 at other places in Egypt. Some have stepped sides and bent tops.

• This is what the Great Pyramid looks like inside.

Who were the ancient Greeks?

The ancient Greeks were people who lived from around 3,000 B.C. to 140 B.C. They didn't live only in Greece—some of them lived to the north and the east, in lands that we now call Bulgaria and Turkey. Others lived on small rocky islands in the Aegean Sea.

• Many Greeks set sail for North Africa, Turkey, Italy, and France. They found safe harbors where they built new towns, and they cleared the land for farming.

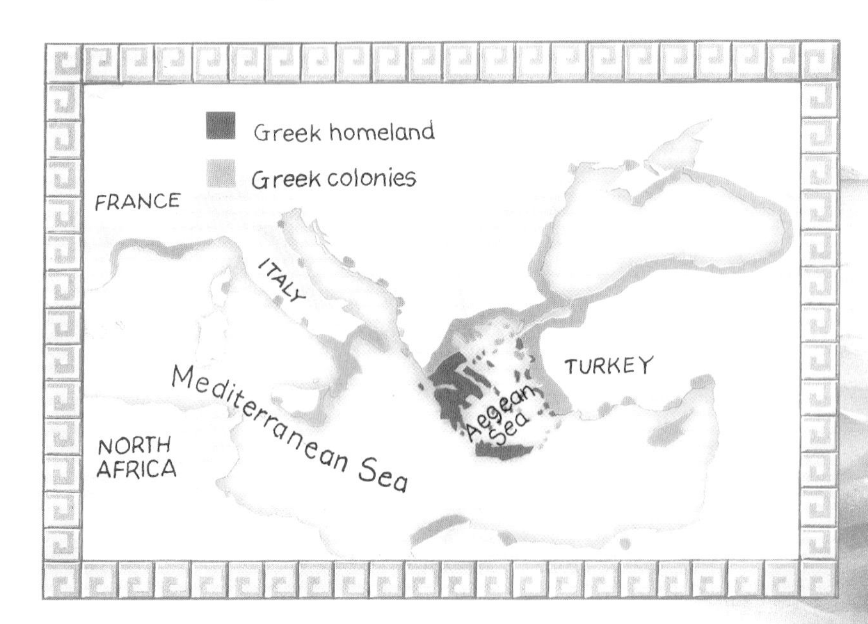

• By 500 B.C. the Greek world was large, rich, and powerful. It stretched from France in the west to Turkey in the east.

• Wherever they went, the Greek settlers took their own way of life. They must have looked strange to the locals!

• The Greeks were smart people. They had good laws and strong armies. They built beautiful temples and theaters. They were great thinkers, artists, and athletes.

Why did Greece grow bigger and bigger?

Greece started off as a small country, and much of its land was too rocky for farming. By about 750 B.C., there was little room left for new towns or farms, and food began to run short. Because of this, many people left Greece to look for new places to live, and the Greek world began to grow.

Who was goddess of wisdom?

Athena was the goddess of war and also of wisdom—her symbol was the wise owl. She had special powers to protect the city of Athens, too, and the citizens loved and worshiped her. They built Athena a temple, called the Parthenon, high on the Acropolis—a hill overlooking the city.

• According to legend, the gods lived on top of Mount Olympus, the highest mountain in Greece. But they didn't always behave as you'd expect gods to —they spent a lot of their time quarreling!

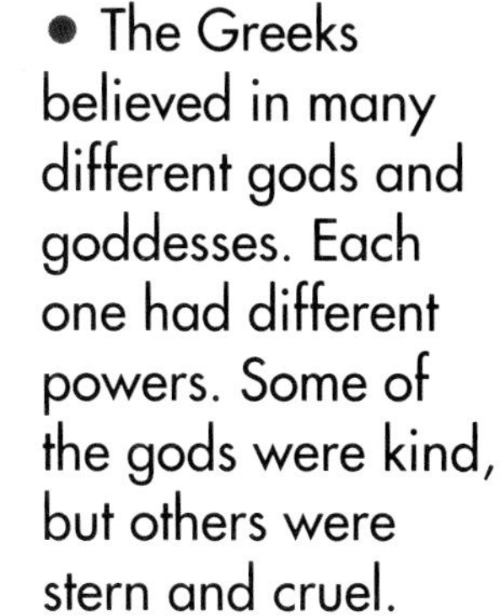

• The Greeks believed in many different gods and goddesses. Each one had different powers. Some of the gods were kind, but others were stern and cruel.

Who told stories about the gods?

A famous poet named Homer told exciting stories about gods and heroes. His poem *The Odyssey* tells of Odysseus, a Greek soldier sailing home to Ithaca from the war with Troy. The sea god Poseidon tries to sink his ship, but with Athena's protection, Odysseus finally gets home.

• **Poseidon**, god of the sea, tried to sink Odysseus's ship by stirring up violent storms.

• Inside the Parthenon stood a towering statue of Athena—about ten times taller than you! It was covered with gold and ivory.

Who were the Romans?

The Romans were people who lived in Rome more than 2,000 years ago. They became very powerful. By A.D. 100, they had conquered the lands around them and ruled a huge empire. It was one of the mightiest empires in the ancient world.

• Different parts of the empire had very different climates. The Romans boiled in Egypt, where the summers were sweltering...

• An old legend says that the city of Rome was first started by a man named Romulus. He and his twin brother Remus had been abandoned by their parents and were looked after by a wolf!

Did all the Romans live in Rome?

• ...but they shivered in the icy Swiss Alps and in northern Britain. These were the coldest places in the whole empire.

The city of Rome wasn't big enough for all the Romans! In total, there were about 50 million people in the empire, which stretched from Britain in the north to Africa in the south. Everyone in the empire was protected by Rome's armies and had to obey Rome's laws.

THE ROMAN EMPIRE A.D. 100

Caspian Sea
Black Sea
Constantinople
ASIA MINOR
Athens
Ephesus
Antioch
SYRIA
Mediterranean Sea
ARABIA
Alexandria
EGYPT
Red Sea
N

• It would have taken nearly 100 days to travel on horseback across the whole of the empire. It was a journey of about 3,000 miles.

Where can you visit a Roman town?

Pompeii was a bustling town not far from Rome. In A.D. 79, a nearby volcano erupted, burying the town in ash. Pompeii lay hidden for centuries until, one day, some farmers discovered its Roman remains. Today you can visit Pompeii to find out about life in Roman times.

• Archaeologists have studied Pompeii since the 1800s and have uncovered an almost perfect Roman town.

MAKING MODELS

1. People were buried by the ash. Over the years, their bodies rotted away, leaving people-shaped holes in the hardened ash or rock.

2. Archaeologists used the holes as molds. They poured plaster inside and waited for it to set.

3. Chipping away at the rock left plaster models of the Romans. Archaeologists study these carefully to learn about Roman life.

• The Roman Empire grew weaker and weaker. It was attacked by warriors from the north and the east, who split up the empire into many small kingdoms.

• Mount Vesuvius was an active volcano. As it erupted, showers of ash poured onto Pompeii, killing the people with poisonous fumes.

How do we know about the Romans?

The Roman Empire came to an end in the 470s. Yet many Roman buildings, mosaics, writings, paintings, and weapons have survived. These remains tell us a lot about the Romans and how they lived.

• Some Roman finds are very peculiar. Archaeologists in London have dug up a pair of black leather underpants. Who could have lost them all those years ago?

What were the Middle Ages in the middle of?

We call the years between the ancient world and the modern world in Europe the Middle Ages. They started in the 470s, when rule by the Romans came to an end, and they ended in the 1450s.

• The Romans once ruled most of Europe and North Africa. Then fierce warriors invaded, splitting Roman lands into many small kingdoms. By the 1450s Europe had larger countries again, more like those of today.

• The map above includes the people and places talked about in this book.

• In the Middle Ages, no one knew what the whole world looked like.

This is what Arab mapmakers thought the world looked like in the 1150s. It shows Asia, North Africa, and Europe. Neither the Arabs nor the Europeans knew about other parts of the world.

Most people thought the world was flat. Sailors had to be brave to go on long voyages — they were afraid of falling over the edge!

Why did castles have moats?

Moats were deep wide ditches filled with water, which made it harder for enemies to break into a castle. Friendly visitors could cross the moat over a drawbridge. But when enemies attacked, the drawbridge was raised.

• Spies and traitors were chained up in the castle's dungeons. These were dark and damp and full of rats and spiders!

• One way to beat enemies who shut themselves up in a castle was to surround it — and wait! This was called a siege. When the castle ran out of food and water, the people inside had to give in.

• Strong stone walls were built to protect towns and cities all over the world. The picture on the right shows Great Zimbabwe, a walled city begun in the 1000s by the Shona people of southern Africa.

• Pueblo Bonito was one of the walled towns built by the Anasazi people of North America between 950 and 1300.

• In the 1300s, people in Europe learned how to make big guns called cannons. In time it became easier to blow up castles — if the guns went off properly!

Why did knights wear armor?

In battle, knights were bashed and battered by swords, arrows, axes, long pointed lances, and metal clubs called maces. They had to protect their bodies from all these sharp weapons, so they wore suits of tough metal armor.

• Until the 1200s most knights wore chainmail armor. This was made from linked metal rings. Later armor was made from solid metal plates.

By the end of the Middle Ages, a knight was like a can of beans on legs completely covered with metal!

• Putting on armor wasn't easy. A squire was a boy who was learning to be a knight. He helped the knight get ready for battle.

Armor wasn't very comfortable to wear, so knights put on thick padded clothes underneath.

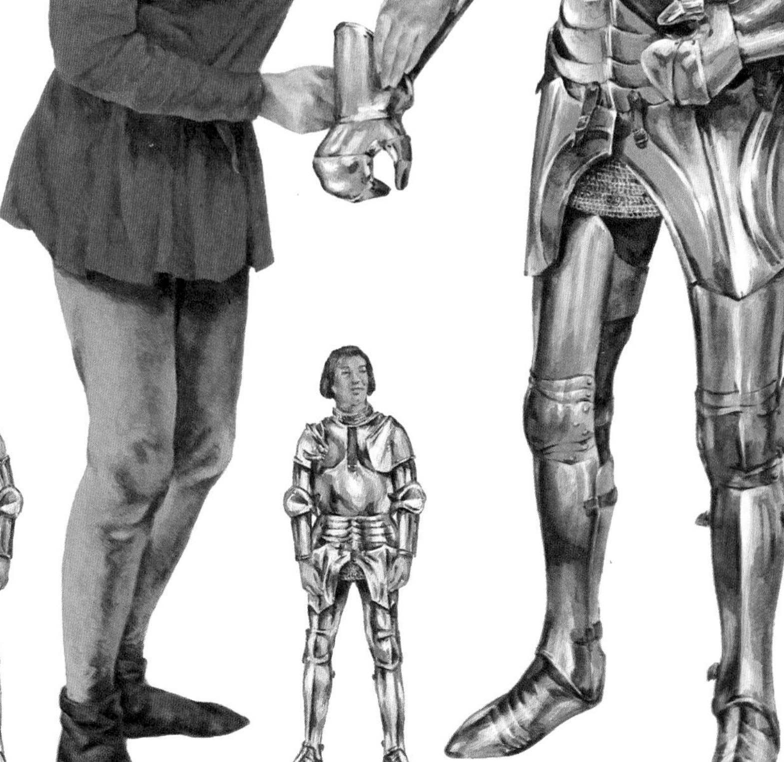

• Japanese knights were called samurai. Their armor was made of metal plates attached to padded silk and leather.

• Bows and deadly arrows were used by soldiers in most parts of the world.

Welsh longbowman

Turkish crossbowman

Aztec warrior

Mongol archer

• A samurai always had a bath before going into battle. Then, if he died, he knew he would be clean and ready to go to heaven.

Where was Vinland?

Viking sailors from Scandinavia were the first Europeans to cross the Atlantic Ocean and reach North America. They landed on the east coast in the early 1000s and named it Vinland, or Vineland, because they found lots of grapevines there.

• No one is quite certain where Vinland was, but the most likely place is Newfoundland, in what is Canada today. People now think the Vikings found cranberries or gooseberries there, not grapes!

Who went to sea in junks?

By the 1400s, Chinese junks were the world's biggest ships. The largest were five times the size of ships being built in Europe.

• A Moroccan called Ibn Batuta spent 30 years traveling. He went east to India, China, and Sumatra, and south to Timbuktu, in Africa. He lived in the 1300s.

• One of the great explorers of the Middle Ages was a Venetian named Marco Polo. It took him four whole years to travel to China.

• Polynesian sailors explored the vast South Pacific Ocean in nothing bigger than canoes. The Maoris are descended from Polynesians who reached New Zealand about 1,000 years ago.

Was Sinbad a real sailor?

The exciting adventures of Sinbad the Sailor were folktales made up by Persian storytellers in the Middle Ages. Although Sinbad was make-believe, there were lots of real people making amazing journeys over land and across the ocean.

Where did Robin Hood live?

The stories about Robin Hood say he lived in Sherwood Forest, near the English town of Nottingham. He and his Merry Men were outlaws, because they broke the law by robbing the rich, but they gave the money to poor people.

• Was there really such a person as Robin Hood? Nobody knows for sure. Some people think he was an outlaw called Robert Fitzooth, the Earl of Huntingdon.

• People have told stories about Robin Hood, Maid Marian, and the Merry Men since the 1300s.

• Everyone enjoys a good story. Today we can look at books or watch movies and videos. In the Middle Ages, people loved to listen to storytellers.

Who was Joan of Arc?

Joan was a French peasant girl who grew up at a time when England and France were at war. In 1429, at the age of 17, she dressed up as a soldier and helped to free the city of Orleans from an English army. But just a year later she was captured and burned at the stake.

Who was a teenage warrior?

Temujin was the son of a leader of the Mongol people of central Asia. He was born in 1162 and he became a warrior when he was only 13, after his father died. He took the name Genghis Khan. Under his leadership, the Mongols attacked and won many lands in Asia.

Who were the Tudors?

The Tudors were kings and queens who ruled England for nearly 200 years. They were called the Tudors because Tudor was their last name. The most famous of them was Henry VIII, who ruled during the 1500s.

• The *Mary Rose* was the pride and joy of Henry's navy. A fortune was spent on doing it up, but when the royals went to see it set out it sank before it even left the port!

• The rich wore clothes of velvet and lace, with pearls or other precious jewels sewn on. They looked beautiful, but they smelled terrible—they hardly ever took a bath!

• Henry VIII was the first head of the Church of England. He closed down the Catholic monasteries and spent their riches on his wars, or on building new manor houses.

● The Spanish sent a fleet of ships to invade England in 1558. Francis Drake, the head of the English navy, had no worries that the Spanish would win. He even finished the game of bowls he was playing before he went to fight them!

What happened to the Aztecs?

The Aztecs were a rich and powerful people who lived in Mexico. But they were defeated by Hernán Cortés in 1521. He ransacked their cities for gold and other riches, which he took back to the Queen of Spain.

● Queen Elizabeth I was the last of the Tudors. She never married so when she died, her distant cousin, James VI of Scotland, became king of England too. His last name was Stuart, so the next group of rulers were called the Stuarts.

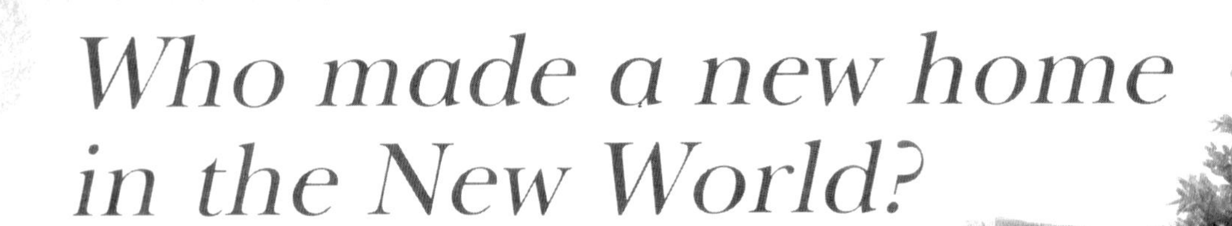

Who made a new home in the New World?

In 1620, English settlers sailed to America on the *Mayflower*. These settlers are sometimes called the Pilgrim Fathers, but there were actually whole families on the ship! The Pilgrims wanted to start a new life in America and they became the first colonists in New England.

- Every year, we remember the Pilgrims' first harvest when we celebrate Thanksgiving Day.

- Winters were hard and the Pilgrims' crops failed, but nearby tribes showed them how to grow new crops like corn and potatoes.

• The Pilgrims left England because they weren't happy with the king. They weren't the only ones! In 1605 there'd been a plot to blow him up when he opened Parliament—the Gunpowder Plot.

Who built the best home for the next world?

The Taj Mahal is a magnificent tomb in India. The Mogul ruler Shah Jahan built it for his favorite wife, who died in 1629. It was made of white marble and took 21 years to build. The outside is decorated with flowers and passages from the Muslim holy book, *The Koran*.

• The explorer Christopher Columbus discovered America in 1492. No one had ever sailed so far west. Some people thought he might fall off the edge of the world!

Who was the "last" king of France?

Louis XVI was a French king. He and his queen lived extravagantly—and paid for it by taxing the people. Finally the people rebelled and the king and queen were put in prison and later executed. Many years later France went back to having kings for a short time but today it has a president like the U.S.A.

• Queen Marie Antoinette of France was spoiled and rich. When she was told there was no bread for the starving peasants, she couldn't see why they didn't eat cake instead!

• Louis XVI and his queen both had their heads chopped off, by a new machine called a guillotine.

• The final straw for the French was the "gabelle." This new tax made salt too expensive for most people. And in the days before refrigerators, salt was about the only way to keep meat fresh.

• President Washington's head can still be seen on coins and bills today.

• The United States had to fight to become free, or independent, of Britain. The war was called the Revolutionary War.

Who was the first president of the United States?

George Washington became the first president of the United States in 1789. Before then, the British king had ruled America—from nearly 3,000 miles across the the ocean.

• The American people were fed up with paying taxes to the British king. One night a few of them ransacked a British tea ship in Boston harbor and threw all the tea chests overboard. We call it the Boston Tea Party—some party!

Who steamed into the twentieth century?

Many of today's machines were invented in the 1800s. Factories were built and people grew richer. It was cheaper and quicker to make things, such as clothes. Today we call this time the Industrial Revolution, because there were so many changes in industry.

• Inventions like the new steam trains changed everyone's lives. It meant more people could afford to travel.

• The Great Exhibition of 1851 in London showed off all the new goods that were being made. Even the building was amazing —the Crystal Palace was built entirely of glass and iron.

• All this industry needed power, which came from coal. Even children worked in the coal mines—because they were small they could get into the tiniest tunnels.

• Families were a lot bigger in the 1800s than they are today. Many families had ten children or even more!

COUNTRIES AND PEOPLES

What is a country?

A country is an independent land with its own government. The government runs the country, and makes laws which the people must keep. A country has its own name, and its borders are normally agreed by other countries around the world.

• Each country has its own money, called currency, with its own style of coins and bills. There are rubles in Russia and francs in France.

• All countries have their own stamps, which often carry a picture of the country's ruler. Some stamps show a country's wildlife, or mark an important discovery.

• People wave their national flags at parades, sports events, and celebrations.

Why do countries fly flags?

Every country has its own flag, which is a sort of national emblem. Each country's flag is different. The design may include colored stripes, star and sun patterns, or religious signs such as crosses or crescents. Flags are flown on special occasions, as a symbol of a country and its people.

• Every country has its own special song called a national anthem. This is sung to show respect for a country and its history.

How many countries are there?

There are about 190 independent countries in the world, but the number changes from year to year. This is because new countries are sometimes made, or two countries may join together, as East and West Germany did in 1990.

1 Guatemala
2 Belize
3 El Salvador
4 Honduras
5 Nicaragua
6 Costa Rica
7 Panama
8 Cuba
9 Bahamas
10 Jamaica
11 Haiti
12 Dominican Republic
13 Antigua and Barbuda
14 Dominica
15 Barbados
16 St. Vincent and the Grenadines
17 Trinidad and Tobago
18 Ecuador
19 Ireland
20 United Kingdom
21 Belgium
22 Netherlands
23 Luxembourg
24 Switzerland
25 Liechtenstein
26 San Marino
27 Vatican City
28 Italy
29 Monaco
30 Andorra
31 Denmark
32 Estonia
33 Latvia
34 Lithuania
35 Czech Republic
36 Austria
37 Slovakia
38 Hungary
39 Slovenia
40 Croatia
41 Bosnia and Herzogovina
42 Yugoslavia
43 Macedonia
44 Albania
45 Greece
46 Bulgaria
47 Moldova
48 Malta
49 Cyprus
50 Lebanon
51 Israel
52 Jordan
53 Armenia
54 Azerbaijan
55 Kuwait
56 Bahrain
57 Qatar
58 United Arab Emirates

• Some small Pacific island countries are not shown on this map: Fiji, Kiribati, Marshall Islands, Federated States of Micronesia, Nauru, Palau, Tonga, Tuvalu, and Western Samoa.

59 Tajikistan
60 Kyrgyzstan
61 Bhutan
62 Bangladesh
63 Sri Lanka
64 Singapore
65 Brunei
66 Eritrea
67 Djibouti
68 Uganda
69 Rwanda
70 Burundi
71 Malawi
72 Zimbabwe
73 Swaziland
74 Lesotho
75 Equatorial Guinea
76 Togo
77 Liberia
78 Sierra Leone
79 Guinea
80 Guinea-Bissau
81 Gambia
82 Senegal
83 Burkina Faso
84 Tunisia

Which country has the most people?

Well over a billion people live in China, and about 48,000 new babies are born there every day. You'd think that meant a lot of birthdays, but in China everyone celebrates their birthday at the same time—the Chinese New Year!

• Chinese New Year is celebrated by Chinese people all over the world in late January or early February. There are spectacular street processions.

• In July 1991, both the U.S.A. *and* Canada celebrated their birthdays—over 75,000 people showed up to a huge party, held in the U.S.A.

Which is the biggest country?

Russia is so big it takes eight days to cross it by train! As children set off for school in the capital, Moscow, in the west, others are already going home in the eastern port of Vladivostok.

Where is there land, but no countries?

The vast frozen land around the South Pole is called Antarctica. It is not a country—it has no people, no government, and no flag. Many countries have signed an agreement promising to keep Antarctica as a wilderness for scientists to study.

- Nobody lives in Antarctica except for a few hundred scientists, who go there to study rocks, the weather, and plant and animal life.

Where are there only two seasons?

Many tropical countries have only two seasons in the year. One is very wet and the other very dry. Not many trees manage to survive the dry months, and animals travel hundreds of miles searching for food and water.

• Many animals migrate in different seasons. Every year, swarms of monarch butterflies leave Mexico and fly 2,000 miles to spend the summer beside cool Canadian lakes.

• During the dry season, the ground is baked hard by the hot sun. Clouds of dust cover everything and everyone.

• In the dry season, herds of wildebeest and zebra cross the grasslands of central Africa. They follow the thunderclouds in search of rainwater and fresh grass.

• Tropical lands lie near the equator. They are the warmest parts of the Earth.

Where does it pour for a month?

Some parts of India and Southeast Asia have long, heavy downpours called monsoons. Big black clouds are blown in from the sea during the summer months. Once the rain starts, it can last for weeks, flooding the fields and streets.

Which city is above the clouds?

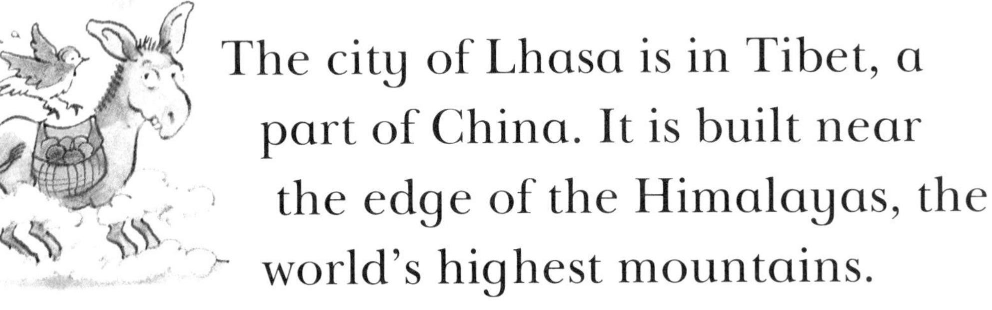

The city of Lhasa is in Tibet, a part of China. It is built near the edge of the Himalayas, the world's highest mountains. Lhasa is so high that it's often covered by clouds, which blanket the city in a thick wet mist!

- Some people call Tibet the Roof of the World, because it so high up in the mountains.

Why do Venetians walk on water?

The Italian city of Venice is built on dozens of tiny islands in a sheltered lagoon near the sea. In between the islands are canals, which form the main "streets" of the city. To get from one part of Venice to another, you don't take a bus or a train —you catch a motorboat or a gondola.

• A country's capital city is where the government works. Washington, D.C. is the capital of the U.S.A. The president lives there, in the White House.

• You have to climb 1,000 steps to reach the Potala Palace, which towers above the streets of Lhasa. It's very grand —even its roofs are made of gold!

Which is the world's biggest city?

Over 21 million people live in Mexico's capital. Mexico City is already home to more people than the whole of Australia, and it's growing fast!

Who rides on a snowmobile?

• A dog team can pull a sled about 50 miles in a day. A snowmobile covers that distance in an hour.

Many of the people who live in icy parts of North America travel across the frozen snow on powerful sleds called snowmobiles. Not long ago, sleds were pulled by husky dogs, but now these are only raced for fun.

• Trains in Tokyo, Japan, are so crowded that railroad staff called crushers have to push in the passengers while the doors close.

• Fishermen in Portugal paint "magic" eyes on their boats to watch over them at sea and bring them safely to harbor.

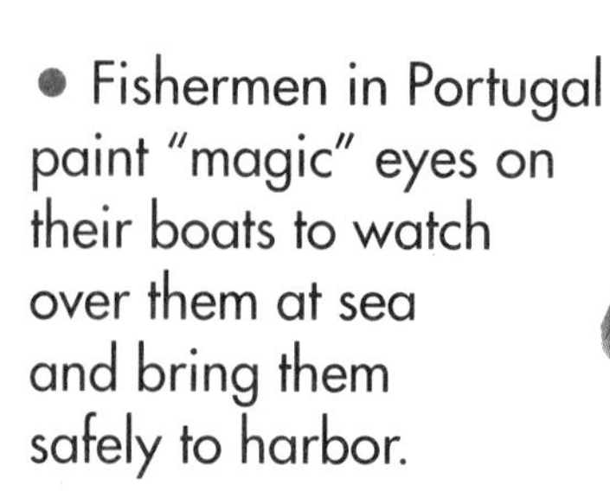

Where do you park your bike in China?

There are millions and millions of people in China, and many millions of bikes! All Chinese cities have huge parking lots for bikes. An attendant gives your bike a number, and helps you to find it again later.

Who paints pictures on trucks?

The truck drivers of Afghanistan are very proud of their trucks. They paint pictures all over them, covering every last inch with bright, colorful patterns. Even the wheel nuts are painted different colors.

• The Afghans may drape their trucks with silver chains and even stick on ring-pulls from soda cans as decorations.

Who writes with a paintbrush?

• The art of beautiful handwriting is called calligraphy. Japanese children learn calligraphy at school.

永 In China and Japan handwriting can be an art. Instead of writing with a pen, people sometimes paint words slowly and beautifully with a brush and ink. Artists often frame their written work, and hang it on the wall just like a picture.

• About 50,000 different symbols may be used to write Chinese. Luckily, schoolchildren only have to learn about 5,000 of them.

Who reads back-to-front?

To read a book in Arabic or Hebrew, you have to work from right to left. So if this book were in Arabic, the first page would be where the index is now.

Which country speaks over 800 languages?

Papua New Guinea is a land of many languages. Most of the people live in small villages, deep in the rain forest or high up in the misty mountains. Some are so cut off from each other that their languages are quite different.

• In many areas of Papua New Guinea, people can only talk to each other through a translator.

• Around 5,000 languages are spoken throughout the world. Here are just a few ways to say "hello."

• There's a place in New Zealand with 85 letters in its name. And there's another in France with just one!

Which is the oldest dish on the menu?

• All over the world, people pound grains such as corn to make flour for their pancakes.

Pancakes may be the oldest dish of all. Even Stone Age people baked them! The basic recipe—milk, eggs, and flour—is the same the world over, but the kind of flour changes from place to place. Pancakes can be made using flour from potatoes, corn, wheat, or oats.

• In different parts of the world you might find almost anything on your plate—from crunchy insects or chewy snails to snakes, guinea pigs, or even sheep's eyes!

Who eats shells, butterflies, and little worms?

• Table manners vary from place to place. We think it is impolite to put your elbows on the table at dinner, while the French think it's perfectly all right!

We do! These are all types of pasta—their Italian names are *conchiglie* (kon-**chil**-ee—shells), *farfalle* (far-**fal**-ay—butterflies), and *vermicelli* (vur-me-**chel**-ee—little worms).

Vermicelli

Farfalle

Conchiglie

Pasta is a dough made from flour and water, which is cut into shapes and then boiled.

• Pasta dough comes in more than 100 shapes and sizes including stars, snail shapes, and all the letters of the alphabet.

Where does it take all afternoon to have a cup of tea?

In Japan there's a special ancient tea ceremony called *chanoyu* (cha-**noy**-yu). The tea is made so slowly, and sipped so carefully, that it really does take hours. It's not a good idea to show up feeling thirsty!

Where are wheat fields bigger than countries?

The rolling grasslands of Canada and the United States are planted with wheat as far as the eye can see. One Canadian wheat field was so big, it was double the size of the European country San Marino!

• Huge combine harvesters have to work in teams to harvest the gigantic wheat fields.

• More people eat rice than wheat. Rice plants need to stand in water, and are grown on flooded land called paddies.

Where does chocolate grow on trees?

Chocolate is made from the seeds of the cacao (ka-**cow**) tree. These trees don't grow everywhere—just in the hot, wet parts of South America, Southeast Asia, and West Africa.

Which country has more sheep than people?

• In Thailand, coconut farmers train monkeys to harvest their crop. The monkeys scamper up the trunks of the palm trees and throw down the fruits.

Although there are more than 17 million people in Australia, most live around the coast. In the center people run enormous sheep farms. At the last count, there were 147 million sheep—nearly nine times the number of people!

Where do women wear bowler hats?

• Lake Titicaca, in the Andes Mountains is the highest lake in the world. The people there use reed boats to travel between islands.

In the Andes Mountains of South America, many women wear bowler hats. The hat is now a part of their traditional dress, along with full skirts, brightly-colored llama (**la**-ma)-wool shawls, and ponchos.

• Bowler hats were first made for men, not women! British businessmen began wearing them to work over 100 years ago.

Where do men wear skirts?

On special occasions in the Highlands of Scotland, it's traditional for men to wear kilts. These pleated skirts are made of a woolen, plaid cloth called tartan. Kilts are warm, but they only come down to the knee, so they are worn with a pair of long, woolen socks.

Which dress has no stitches?

The Indian sari is a simple length of cloth, that wraps neatly around a woman's body. It has no stitching, buttons, or zippers and its design hasn't really changed for hundreds of years. Saris are made of bright cottons or shimmering silks, and on a hot day they are very cool and comfortable to wear.

- People who live in desert countries traditionally wear long robes and head cloths to protect them from the heat and dust. In Arctic countries people wrap up warmly in fur-lined parkas.

- In Scotland, each family group has its own tartan, with a particular pattern and color.

Who wears money at a wedding?

At a Greek or Turkish wedding, the guests don't take the bride and groom gifts—they take money instead. At the wedding party, this is pinned all over the couple's clothes. Often there is so much money that they are both completely covered.

• On the island of Madagascar, a man makes a speech to his bride-to-be before she'll marry him. If the speech is no good, he pays a fine and starts again!

• Hindu brides decorate their skin with beautiful, lacy patterns for their wedding day. They use a reddish-brown dye called henna.

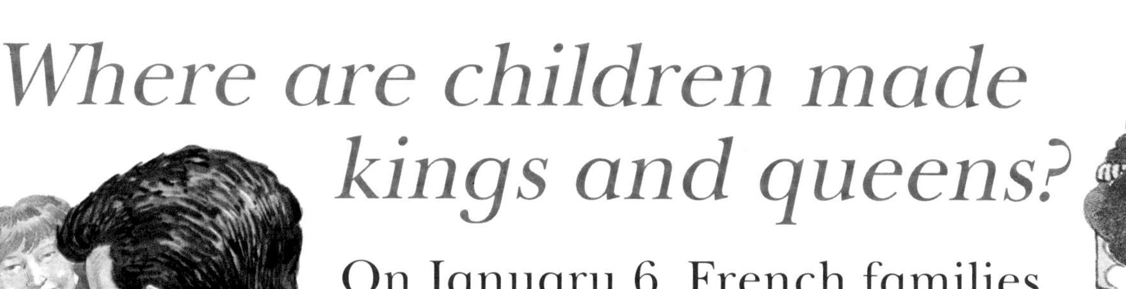

Where are children made kings and queens?

On January 6, French families enjoy a special dinner together. At the end of the meal, the children eat slices of a flat almond pie called a *galette* (ga-**let**). In one slice a charm is hidden. Whoever finds it is crowned king or queen for the night.

• Three kings from the East are said to have visited the two-week-old infant Jesus on January 6.

Who sticks out their tongue to say "hello"?

One of the customs of the Maori people of New Zealand is to welcome important guests by staring at them fiercely, and sticking out their tongues—not something you should try unless you're a Maori!

Who lights the lamps at New Year?

The Hindu New Year is called the Festival of Light—and no wonder! Towns are strung with lights, and lamps shine from every door and window. The women make beautiful floor pictures with colored chalks, flour, and sand, and decorate them with glowing candles.

• Chinese New Year celebrations can last up to 15 days. They begin between the middle of January and the middle of February.

Who brings in the New Year with a bang?

New Year in China starts with beating drums, crashing cymbals, fireworks, and a lion or dragon dancing through the streets. All this noise is meant to chase away the bad days of the past and bring luck in the future.

• The Hindus call their New Year festival Diwali. Diwali falls not in January, but in October or November.

• On New Year's Eve in Ecuador in South America, people burn the Old Year on a bonfire! It's a figure they make from bits of straw.

Who blows a horn at New Year?

The Jewish New Year festival of Rosh Hashanah begins with the blowing of a curly ram's horn. The sound calls people to the synagogue to pray for God's forgiveness for the things they've done wrong in the past year. As the new year begins they can make a fresh start.

• Rosh Hashanah falls in October or November. People eat apples and bread dipped in honey in the hope of a sweet year to come.

Where do elephants glow in the dark?

For the Sri Lankan festival of the Esala Perahera, elephants are decorated with beautiful hangings and strings of electric lights. More than 50 elephants take part in a nighttime procession, along with thousands of drummers and dancers, who crack whips and wave colorful banners.

• The leprechaun (**lep**-re-kon) of Irish folktales is a little green man. The green shamrock is Ireland's national flower.

When do people eat green food?

Saint Patrick is the patron saint of Ireland, and green is the country's national color. Saint Patrick's Day falls on March 17, and for Irish people everywhere it's a time of wild celebration. Some people even dye party food green!

When is the Day of the Dead?

The Day of the Dead is a Mexican holiday which takes place every year on November 2, All Souls' Day. People remember dead friends and relatives by taking flowers and candles to their graves, and having picnics there.

• Brightly painted fake skeletons are made for the Day of the Dead celebrations.

• February is carnival time in many countries, with glittering parades and music.

• The Esala Perahera procession takes place in Kandy, Sri Lanka, at the time of the July full moon.

Where can you play an oil drum?

In the Caribbean islands, large empty oil drums are made into musical drums called steel drums. The top is hammered into a curved dish-shape. This metal dish is then beaten and "tuned" until the different parts of the steel drum make a number of musical sounds. Some drums can play 30 different notes.

• Steel bands play outside in the streets or on the beach at carnival time.

Who bangs on the bongos?

A drummer in a South American dance band often plays the bongos. He grips the drums between his knees and taps them with his fingers and the palm of his hand. This makes zippy rhythms that soon get you dancing.

Can drums talk?

In Nigeria, talking drums can even tell the news. The kalangu drum's beats are like a secret language that only a few people are able to understand. The drummer tightens or loosens the drum skin to change the sounds.

• The Tinguian people of the Philippines thought that the sound of thunder was the god Kadaklan, pounding on his drum.

• A lion-roar drum sounds rather like a real lion—scary! You don't beat this drum. Instead you pull a stick or strip of leather through a hole in the top, and a growling noise rumbles out.

Where can you find a gamelan?

A gamelan is a kind of orchestra from Indonesia. Drums, gongs, xylophones, and chimes all play together to make a magical tinkling sound. There can be as many as 40 instruments in a gamelan.

• Washboards are just trays to scrub clothes on. But some jazz musicians play them like an instrument. They scrape a stick or thimble across the ridges.

• Gamelan players treat their instruments with great respect.

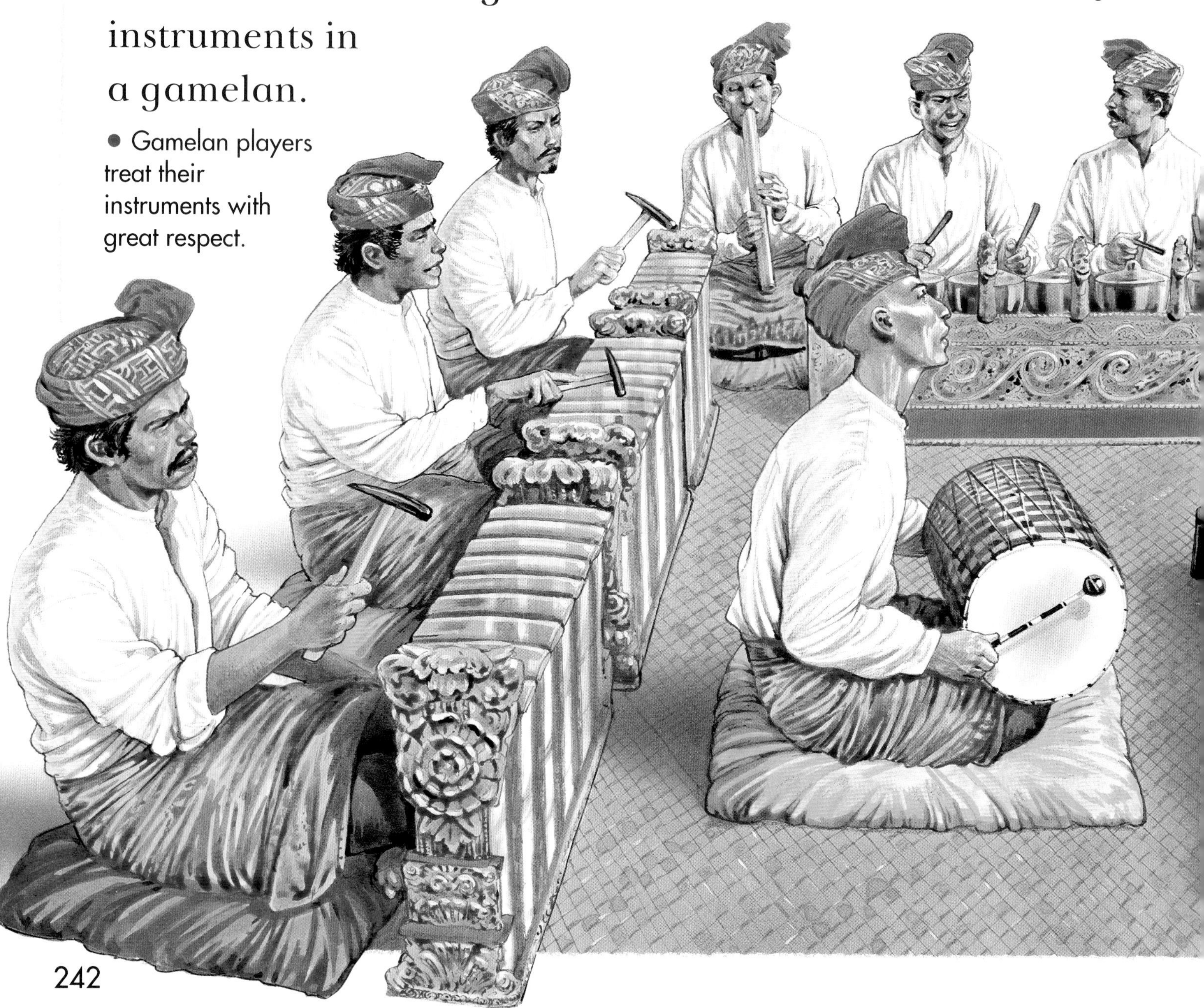

Are rattles just for babies?

Babies aren't the only ones who like the dry, swishing sound rattles make. The first ones were probably dried plant pods, full of seeds. South American rattles called maracas are still often filled with dried beans. You could fill a yogurt tub with some to make your own rattle.

• The triangle is one of the smallest instruments. Larger triangles are used to warn people about fire in some parts of the world, but sirens work better on noisy roads!

What roars like a bull?

The bull-roarer doesn't really roar like an angry bull! It's a block of wood fixed to a piece of string. You whirl it above your head and it makes a strange screaming noise.

How do termites help to make music?

The didgeridoo (dij-uh-ree-**doo**) is a long musical pipe from Australia made from a log of the eucalyptus tree, which is buried inside a termites' mound. The termites gnaw away at the soft wood inside the log, leaving a hollow pipe. Then the pipe is decorated. Didgeridoos can be hollowed out by hand, but they don't give the same rich sound.

Which harp fits inside your mouth?

The tiny Jew's harp doesn't look like its larger cousin. You put it between your teeth, and twang its metal tongue with your finger. It makes your lips feel funny because the metal vibrates so much.

• Didgeridoo-players can breathe in at the same time as they're blowing out through their instrument.

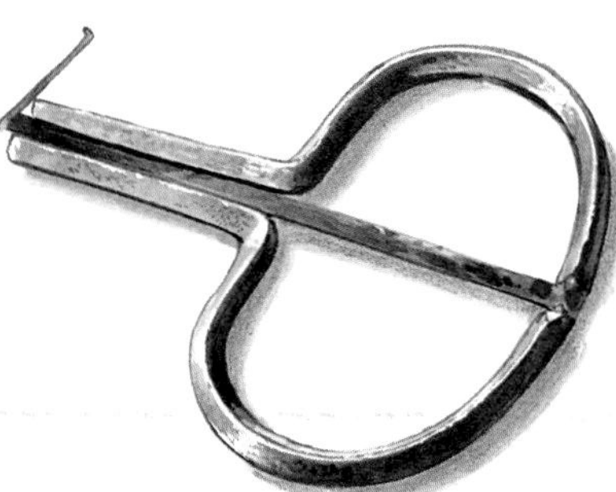

• The Masai people of Kenya play an instrument called a thumb piano. It has metal strips which you pluck with your thumb.

Which instrument is made with a spiderweb?

Take a cow's horn, make a little hole at the pointed end, cover the wide end with a tough kind of spiderweb, and you have a mirliton (**mur**-lee-ton). These are played in Africa. They make a buzzy sound when you blow or sing through them.

• A jazz musician called Roland Kirk could play three saxophones at once! He must have had big lungs!

• Not all bagpipes come from Scotland. This African goatskin bagpipe has been decorated with a carved wooden goat's head!

Where do children watch shadows?

• Javanese puppets are made of painted leather. The puppeteer moves them with wires or rods.

Shadow puppet shows are enjoyed by people all over the world. On the Indonesian island of Java, the audience sits on both sides of a cloth screen. One side watches the puppets, the other sees the shadows dance, as if by magic!

• In a Vietnamese water puppet show, the story is acted out on the surface of a lake. It can't be much fun for the puppeteers—they have to stand in the water.

Who makes pictures from sand?

The Navajo people of the southwestern United States create beautiful pictures with grains of colored sand. The pictures are made on the ground for special ceremonies. But these works of art don't last long—they are destroyed afterward!

• Some sand pictures are said to have healing powers and are big enough to allow the sick person to sit in the middle of them.

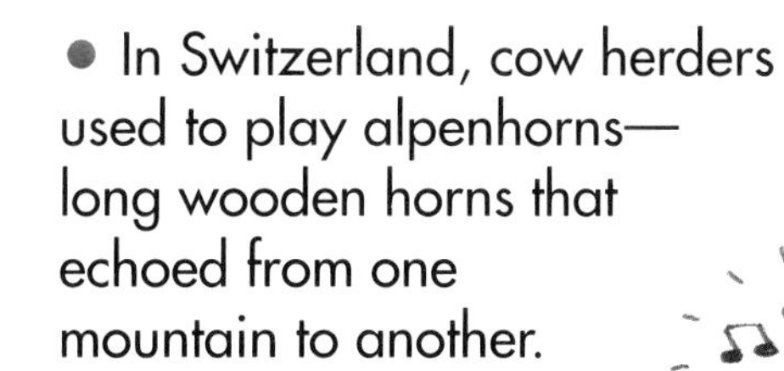

• In Switzerland, cow herders used to play alpenhorns—long wooden horns that echoed from one mountain to another.

Which dancers snap their fingers?

Flamenco dancing comes from southern Spain. Proud-looking dancers toss their heads and snap their fingers, as they stamp and whirl to the music of a Spanish guitar.

Why do people race camels?

• Dromedaries can race at over 12 miles an hour—faster than two-humped camels.

One-humped camels are so sturdy and fast that in hot desert areas they are ridden like racehorses. The races are very popular in Saudi Arabia, and large crowds cheer the camels as they speed across desert racetracks.

• People have been known to race all sorts and sizes of animal—from ostriches to snails!

• The world's fastest ball game is called pelota. The ball is hurled from a wicker scoop at the speed of an express train.

Which is the world's most popular sport?

Soccer balls are kicked around in more than 160 countries around the world. The game is played in playgrounds, parks, streets and, of course, soccer fields.

• The earliest soccer-like game was *zuqiu* (**zoo**-choo). It was played 2,400 years ago in ancient China.

Who lives in a longhouse?

On the tropical island of Borneo, some people live in long, airy buildings that are made of wood and bamboo, and are raised on stilts. These longhouses are home to dozens of different families, each with their own room.

- As many as 100 families may share the same longhouse.

- High-rise apartment buildings are another way of squeezing a lot of homes into a small space. You find them in big towns and cities.

Where do gardens grow on rivers?

In the Netherlands, many people live on barges moored on the country's canals. Boat-owners don't have backyards, of course, but some of them grow flowers on the roof!

How do you stay cozy in the Gobi?

The Gobi Desert is in Mongolia in northern Asia and its winters are icy cold. Some shepherds and their families travel around the desert, living in thick, felt tents called yurts, which keep out the hot sun or the freezing cold.

Could people live in space?

They already have! Some astronauts have lived in space stations spinning around the Earth for as long as a year. There are plans for much bigger stations, where people could live for 10 years, and even for settlements on Mars.

- It would take 8 months to reach Mars in a spacecraft. The crew would have to take everything they needed with them—the food for just one person would make a pile twice as big as a family car.

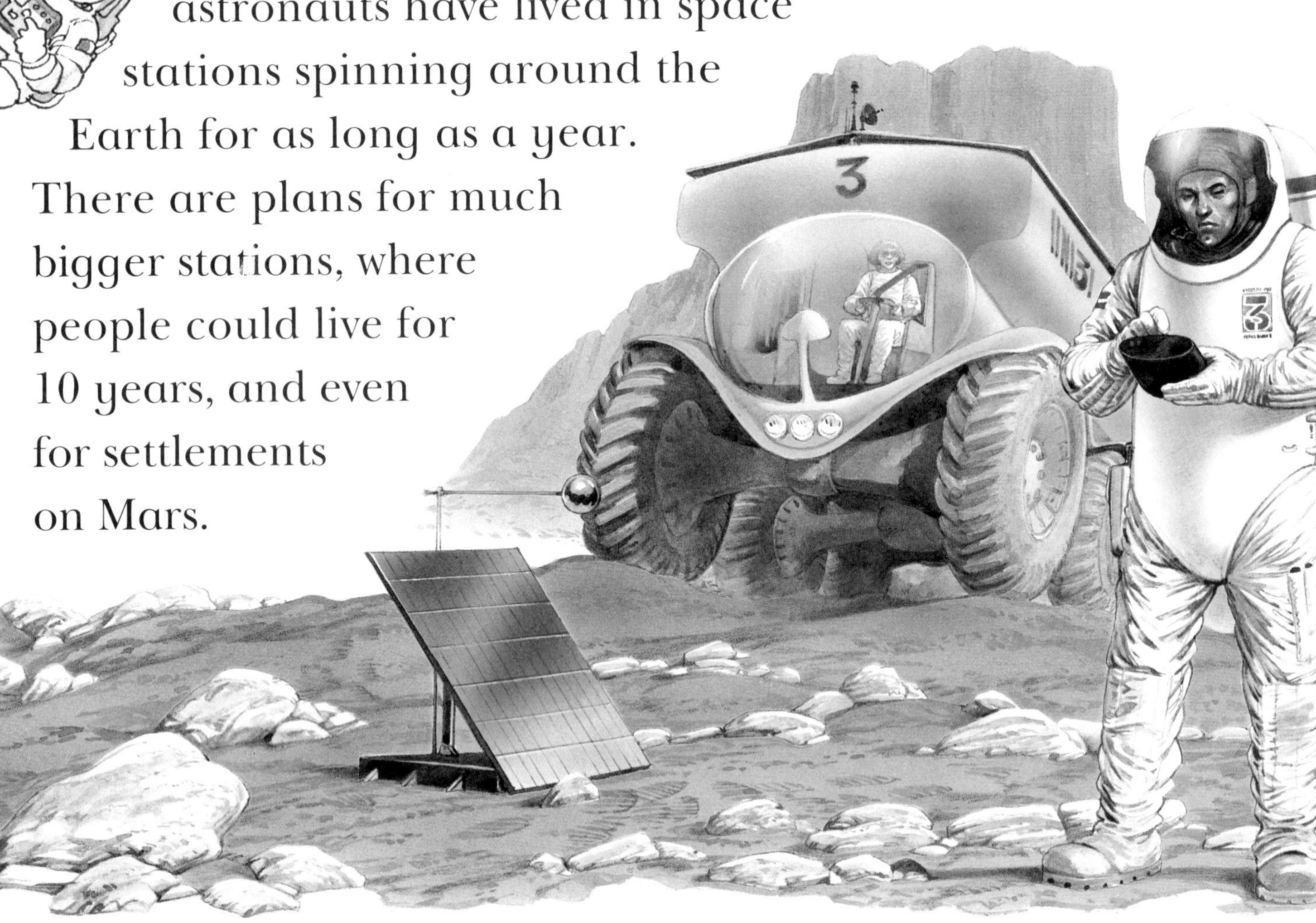

- There are plans for a huge wheel-shaped space station, measuring nearly a mile across.

- People have even lived under the sea, but not for longer than a few weeks at a time. They were working in underwater laboratories.

ANIMALS VOLUME I

• Female Queen Alexandra's birdwings are the world's biggest butterflies. Their wings are almost as big as this page!

• The blue whale is so long that eight elephants could stand along its back.

• The giraffe is the tallest land animal. With its long neck, it can reach as high as a two-story house.

• The mighty African elephant is almost three times as tall as you are. It can weigh as much as seven cars.

• The ostrich is the world's tallest and heaviest bird. It's as tall as a bus!

Which is the biggest animal?

The biggest animal that has ever lived is a mammal — the blue whale. It is even larger than the biggest dinosaurs were. Blue whales can weigh as much as 150 cars!

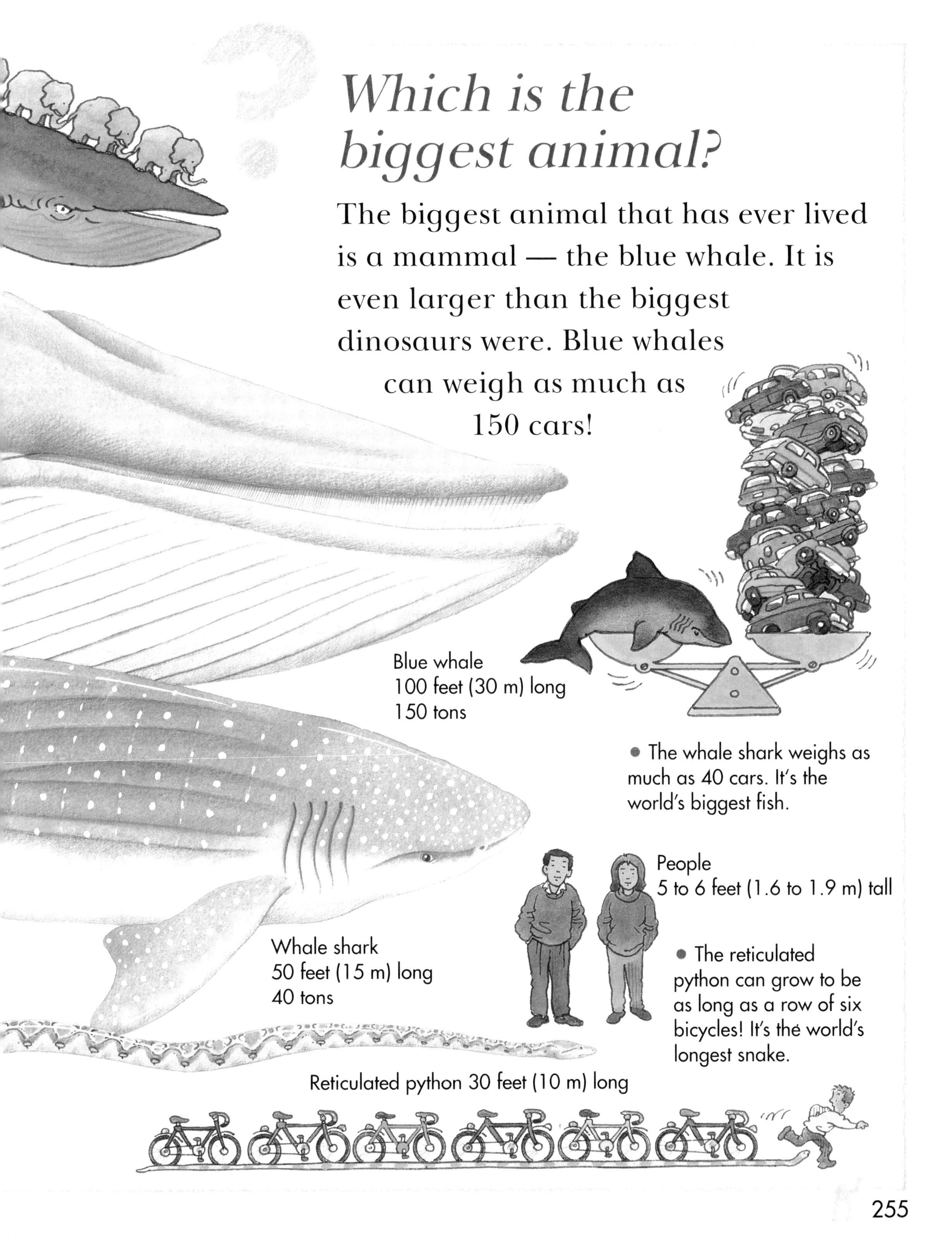

- The whale shark weighs as much as 40 cars. It's the world's biggest fish.

- The reticulated python can grow to be as long as a row of six bicycles! It's the world's longest snake.

What's the difference between sharks and dolphins?

Although sharks and dolphins look alike, they belong to two very different animal groups. Sharks are a kind of fish, but dolphins are members of another group, the mammals.

• You don't look anything like a dolphin, but you are a mammal, too!

• If an animal breathes air through lungs, and its babies feed on their mother's milk, it's a mammal. Most mammals have some fur or hair on their bodies.

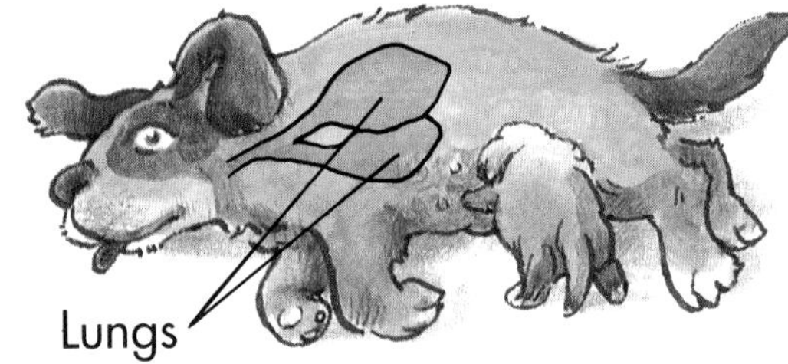

• If an animal has feathers and hatches out of a hard-shelled egg, it's a bird. All birds have wings, and most of them can fly.

• If an animal has six legs and three parts to its body, it's an insect. There are more kinds of insect in the world than all the other kinds of animal put together.

• If an animal has damp slimy skin, and is born in water but lives much of its life on land, it's an amphibian. Baby amphibians hatch out of jellylike eggs.

• If an animal has a dry scaly skin and is born on land, it's a reptile. Most reptiles lay eggs with leathery skins.

• If an animal lives in water, breathes through gills, and uses fins to move, it's a fish. Most fish lay jellylike eggs that hatch into baby fish.

What's the difference between frogs and toads?

Frogs usually have smooth skin and long legs for leaping. Most toads have lumpy skin and move their short thick bodies about by crawling.

...and alligators and crocodiles?

Crocodiles have longer, more pointed snouts than alligators. Crocodiles also have one very large tooth sticking up on each side when they close their mouths.

- Frogs and toads are both amphibians.

- Alligators and crocodiles are reptiles.

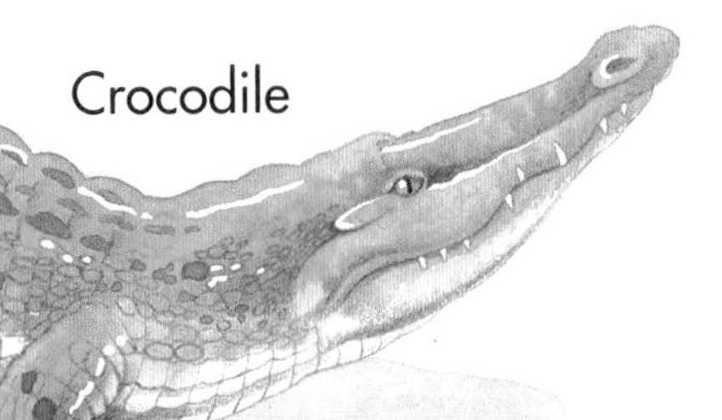

Alligator

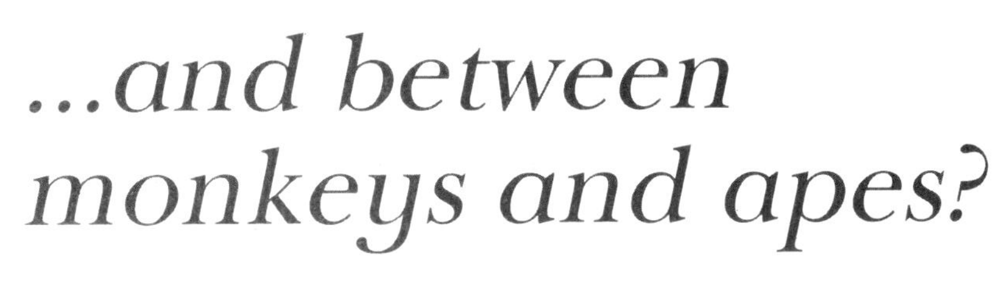

...and between monkeys and apes?

The big difference between these animals is that monkeys have long tails, but apes don't have tails at all. There are lots of different kinds of monkey, but the only apes are gorillas, orangutans, chimpanzees, and gibbons.

Spider monkey

Orangutan (ape)

- Monkeys and apes are mammals

- A woodlouse looks like it's an insect, but it isn't — it has too many legs! This creepy-crawly is related to crabs and lobsters.

- Rabbits and hares are both mammals.

...and rabbits and hares?

Hares have longer legs and ears than rabbits. Their whiskers are longer, too.

Why do animals have skeletons inside their bodies?

Not all animals have skeletons, but most large ones do. This is because the bigger an animal is, the more it needs a strong sturdy framework to hold its body together and carry its weight. Skeletons also protect soft inside parts, like brains and hearts.

- Animals without backbones are called invertebrates. Insects, spiders, snails, worms, jellyfish, shrimps, and crabs are all invertebrates.

- Animals with backbones are called vertebrates. Fish are vertebrates, and so are amphibians, reptiles, birds, and mammals.

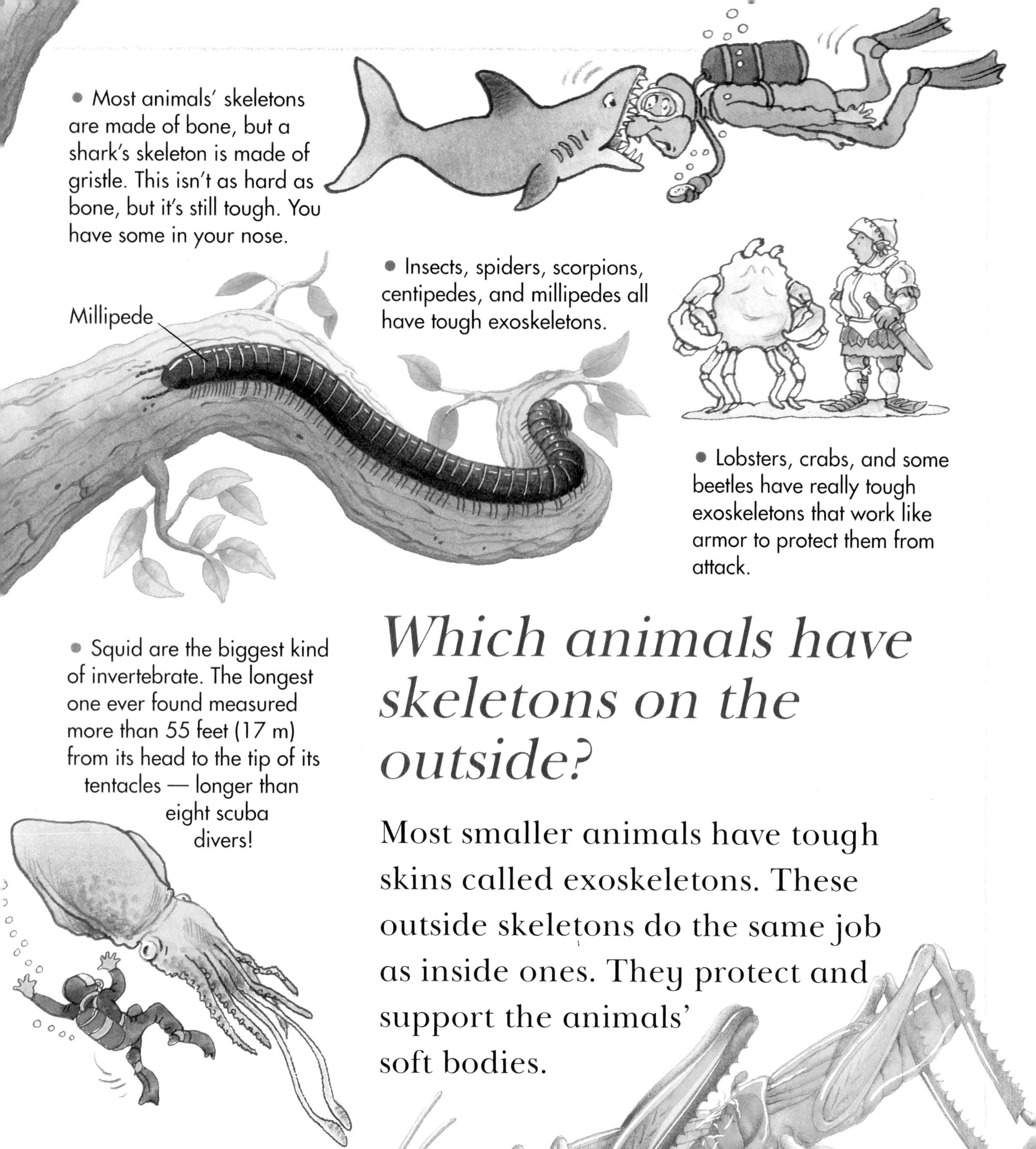

• Most animals' skeletons are made of bone, but a shark's skeleton is made of gristle. This isn't as hard as bone, but it's still tough. You have some in your nose.

• Insects, spiders, scorpions, centipedes, and millipedes all have tough exoskeletons.

• Lobsters, crabs, and some beetles have really tough exoskeletons that work like armor to protect them from attack.

• Squid are the biggest kind of invertebrate. The longest one ever found measured more than 55 feet (17 m) from its head to the tip of its tentacles — longer than eight scuba divers!

Which animals have skeletons on the outside?

Most smaller animals have tough skins called exoskeletons. These outside skeletons do the same job as inside ones. They protect and support the animals' soft bodies.

• To grow larger, an animal has to break out of its old exoskeleton and grow a new one.

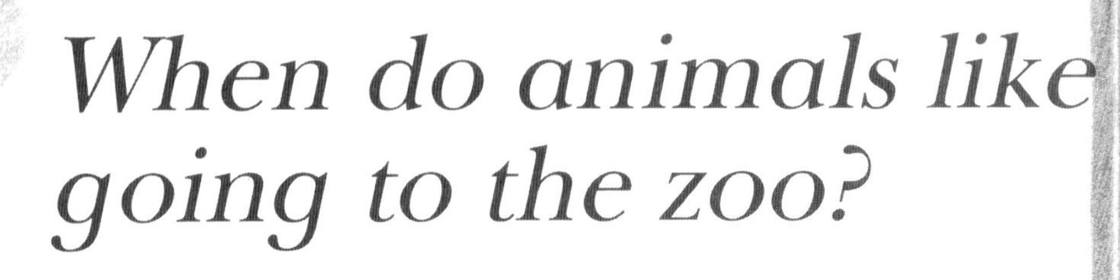

When do animals like going to the zoo?

In the past, zoos kept animals just for people to look at. To some people, the animals looked cramped and lonely. Today, many zoos are working hard to breed endangered animals, such as tamarins, so that they can return them to the wild.

When do animals like leaving the zoo?

The last wild Arabian oryx was shot in 1972—others were rescued and were kept in zoos. They bred and now a herd of more than 100 roams the deserts of Oman once more.

Sixty-five years ago, the golden hamster was nearly extinct. Then one female and her 12 young were caught and allowed to breed in safety. Soon there were millions of them!

Which endangered animal is brought up in a bucket?

Kemp's ridley turtles are being raised in special hatcheries in Texas and Mexico. In their buckets, they are safe from seabirds and other hunters. When they are big enough to fend for themselves they are put into the ocean.

Everyone thought the bridled nailtail wallaby, or flashjack, was extinct. Then a colony was discovered in 1973 near Dingo in eastern Australia. The area where they live is now protected.

Why do animals need us?

In most cases, animals become endangered because of things that people do. Animals cannot speak, so they need us to speak for them. Most of all, they need us to stop doing the harmful things we do and help keep them safe.

- Lots of people are helping animals in danger. If there's an oil spill, for example, teams work hard to clean the animals so that they can be returned to the wild.

- Everyone can help to save endangered animals. We can join groups that are trying to protect them. We can be careful about the things we buy, and we can take less from the natural world and make less mess.

Why do we need animals?

Some wild animals provide us with food, clothing, and other materials. If they disappeared we'd lose those things. Animals make the world a beautiful and interesting place. Doesn't it make sense for us to take care of them?

Many people believe we should save animals just because they exist, and that they have as much right to be on this planet as we do. Shouldn't we treat them with the same kindness as we'd wish for ourselves?

What's it like at the Poles?

The North and South Poles are at the very ends of the Earth. They are freezing cold places with biting winds. Ice and snow stretch as far as the eye can see — not the best place for a vacation!

• Polar bears live at the North Pole, and penguins live at the South Pole. They never get the chance to meet!

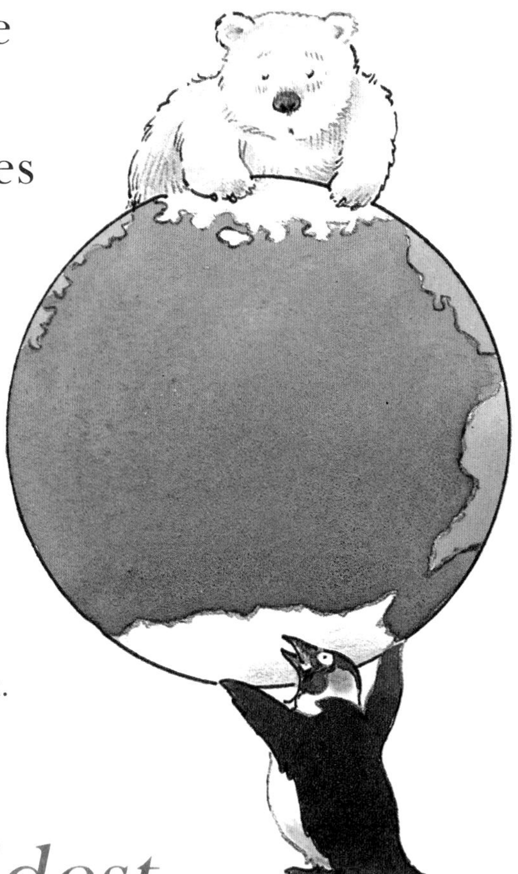

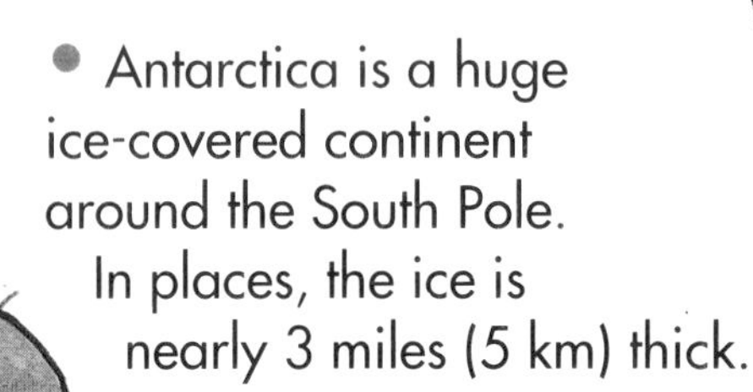

• Antarctica is a huge ice-covered continent around the South Pole. In places, the ice is nearly 3 miles (5 km) thick.

Which is the coldest place in the world?

Vostok Station is a really chilly spot in Antarctica. The temperature here is usually about -72°F (-58°C), but it has dropped to -128°F (-89°C) — the coldest ever known!

• Mount Erebus must be the warmest spot in Antarctica. It's an active volcano!

Where do polar bears live?

Polar bears live around the Arctic Ocean, near the North Pole. Strangely enough, they've never lived in Antarctica, though there's plenty of food and just as much snow and ice there.

• Icebergs float in the sea. They were once part of rivers of ice called glaciers.

• Polar bears never slip on the ice. The rough skin and hair on the soles of their feet give them a bit of extra grip.

Why do camels have humps?

A camel's hump is its own built-in food cupboard. By living off the fat stored in its hump, a camel can go for as long as two weeks without eating. Camels need their humps because they live in deserts, where food and water are hard to find.

Why do elephants have trunks?

An elephant's trunk is a helpful tool. It can be used to pull down leaves and branches to eat. It also makes a good hose — elephants can squirt dust or water over themselves to keep cool.

• Elephants say "hello" to friends by shaking trunks with them.

• An elephant's trunk is a bit like a hand. Using its tip, an elephant can pick up something as small as a button.

• Arabian camels have one hump.

• Bactrian camels have two humps.

• A thirsty camel can drink ten buckets of water in just ten minutes!

Why do giraffes have long necks?

A giraffe's long neck makes it tall enough to eat the leaves at the top of trees. Other animals cannot reach as high, so the giraffe has lots to eat.

• A giraffe's tongue is more than a foot long!

How high can a kangaroo hop?

Believe it or not, big kangaroos can hop right over your head! As far as we know, the highest a kangaroo has ever jumped is about 10 feet (3 m) — more than twice as high as you are tall. Their big, strong back legs help kangaroos to be such good high jumpers.

• For their size, fleas are the world's best high jumpers. They can jump over 100 times their own height.

• By hopping in giant leaps, big kangaroos can move nearly as fast as racehorses!

How fast can a cheetah run?

A hungry cheetah can sprint faster than 60 miles per hour (100 km/h) when chasing something to eat. But running this fast soon wears it out, and it has to stop to get its breath back.

• Cheetahs use their sharp claws to grip and push against the ground as they race along. Olympic runners have spikes on their shoes for the same reason.

• Kangaroos use their tails to balance as they hop. They'd probably fall flat on their faces if they didn't.

Which animal has an extra hand?

Some South American monkeys can grip tree branches with just their tails, leaving their hands free to pick fruit and nuts to eat. Unlike most monkeys, whose tails are completely covered with fur, they have bare skin at the end of their tails — rather like the palm of your hand.

• Sloths are very strange, slow, South American animals. They creep upside down through the treetops, and it can take them a day to move 300 feet (100 m)!

How many ants can an anteater eat?

On a good day, a giant anteater eats an amazing 30,000 ants! It can scoop up as many as 500 with each flick of its long sticky tongue. Anteaters don't munch their food because they don't have any teeth. They swallow the ants whole.

• Giant anteaters have to walk on the knuckles of their front feet because their claws are so long and sharp. They use these claws to rip ant hills apart.

• Birds that feed on fish often have long sharp beaks. The anhinga uses its beak to spear fish.

• Bears tear bees' nests apart to get at the honey inside. They don't seem to mind getting stung.

Which animal uses its finger as a fork?

A strange monkeylike animal called an aye-aye has one finger much longer than the others on each hand. It uses these spindly fingers to poke under tree bark for grubs and insects to eat. Then it skewers them, using its fingers as you would use a fork.

• Aye-ayes only live on the island of Madagascar, off the east coast of Africa.

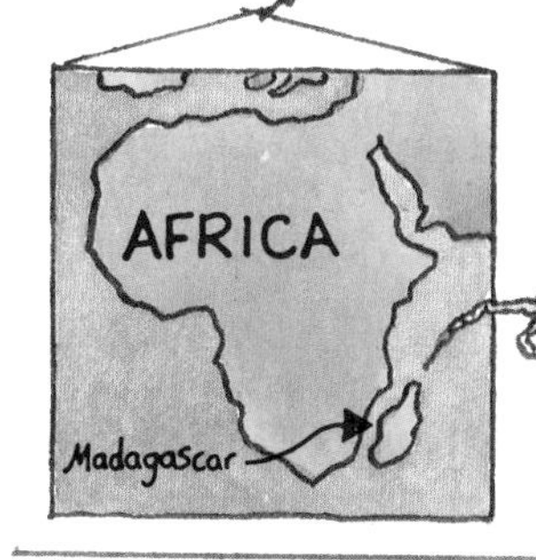

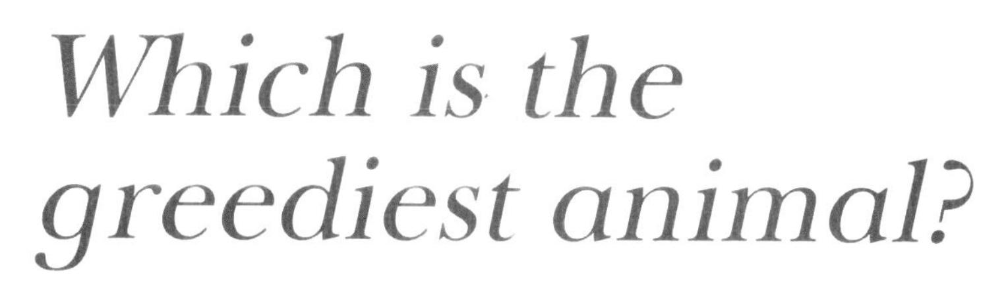

Which is the greediest animal?

For its size, the tiny Etruscan shrew has the world's biggest appetite. It hardly ever stops eating! By the time it's full grown, it has to eat three times its own weight in food each day.

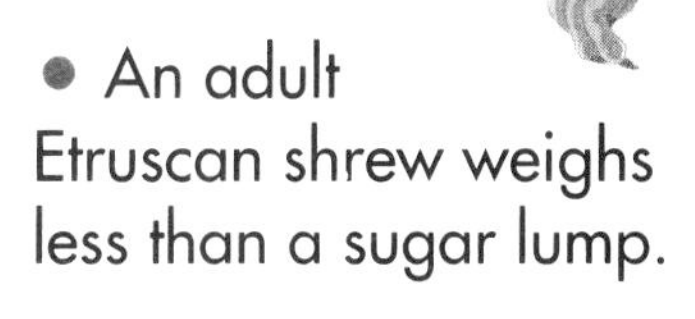

• An adult Etruscan shrew weighs less than a sugar lump.

When does a puppy grow into a dog?

Every puppy is blind and helpless when it's born, but by the time it's two years old it will be fully grown. All pups are roughly the same size when they're born, whatever the type of dog. No wonder it takes smaller types of dogs less time to finish growing up!

2 By six weeks, the puppy is starting to explore. It plays with its brothers and sisters and enjoys a tumble!

1 At about two weeks, the puppy's eyes and ears open. It will begin walking soon.

• A baby wildebeest runs before it can walk! The youngster trots along beside its mother just five minutes after it's born.

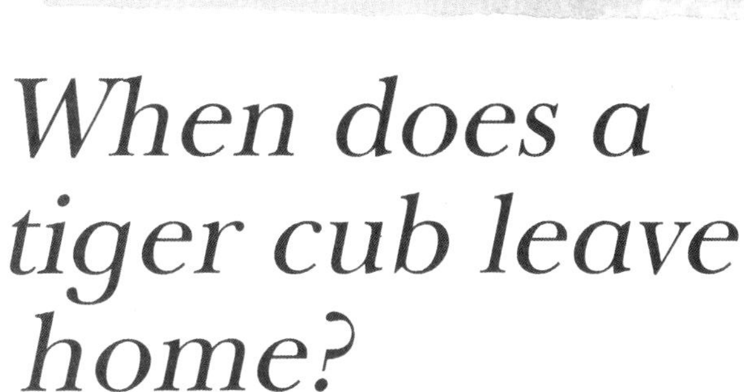

When does a tiger cub leave home?

A mother tiger takes care of her cubs until they're about two years old. But then she has another litter and ignores the older cubs It's not really cruel—the two-year-olds are grown now, and it's about time they took care of themselves.

3 By the time it is full grown, the dog is strong and active. Good food and exercise will help it to stay fit.

• Most insects change shape as they grow. A beetle starts life as a wriggly larva. Then it turns into a pupa. It may not look like it's doing much, but inside the hard skin the insect is changing fast. When it crawls out, it's a full-grown beetle.

Larva

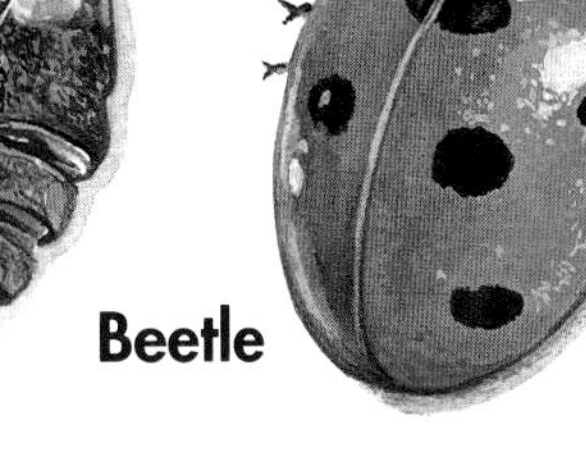

Pupa

Beetle

Which baby is always being washed?

A mother cat licks her kittens from the moment they're born. Licking roughly around the newborn kitten's mouth makes it gasp and start breathing. The mother's tongue dries the kitten's fur too, to keep the kitten warm.

• Flamingos preen their chick's feathers as well as their own. They pick out dirt and insects, and spread oil over the feathers. This oil is produced by the bird's own glands, and makes the feathers waterproof.

• Mud might not seem like a good thing to clean yourself with, but there is nothing a baby hippo likes more than a wallow in a mud bath! And, believe it or not, the mud protects the hippo's skin from the sun and keeps it soft.

Who enjoys a grooming?

A baboon makes sure her babies are well groomed. Working slowly, section by section, she parts the baby's fur and picks carefully with her fingers. She will remove pieces of dead skin, insects, and dirt—and most of what she finds, she eats!

- Sometimes a foal snaps at its mother, but it's only being friendly! The "biting" action is the foal's way of asking its mother to nuzzle it and groom its coat.

Which baby lives in the cleanest nest?

Lots of animals keep their babies' nests clean, but the badger would probably win first prize! Adult badgers regularly line their burrows with fresh dried grass and leaves. They even dig special holes well away from the burrow, which the whole family uses as toilets.

Do snakes have good table manners?

Snakes are not polite at mealtimes. They don't chew a meal, they swallow it whole! They stretch their mouths over their food, until it's all gone. And their jaws and body are so elastic that they can eat things much fatter than themselves.

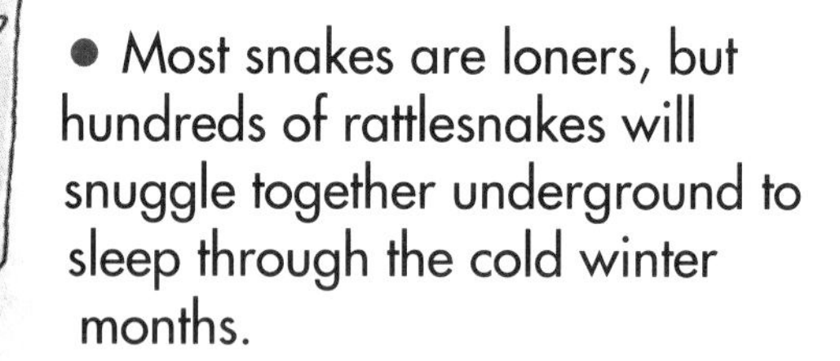

- Most snakes are loners, but hundreds of rattlesnakes will snuggle together underground to sleep through the cold winter months.

- Snakes can bend and twist because their backbones are made up of hundreds of tiny bones, all linked together like a chain.

• An attacking cobra raises its head and spreads out flaps of skin on its head to form a scary-looking hood.

Why do snakes have teeth and fangs?

As well as having teeth to grip its food, a poisonous snake also has a pair of fangs. It uses these long teeth to strike its prey and inject it with poison, which shoots out of holes at the tips of the fangs.

• Vipers have extra-long fangs that fold down flat when they're not in use. It's just as well—the vipers wouldn't be able to shut their mouths otherwise!

Why do snakes stare?

Snakes stare because they can't blink. And they can't blink because they have no eyelids. Each eye is covered with a see-through scale that protects the eye. Snakes get brand-new scales every time they shed their skin.

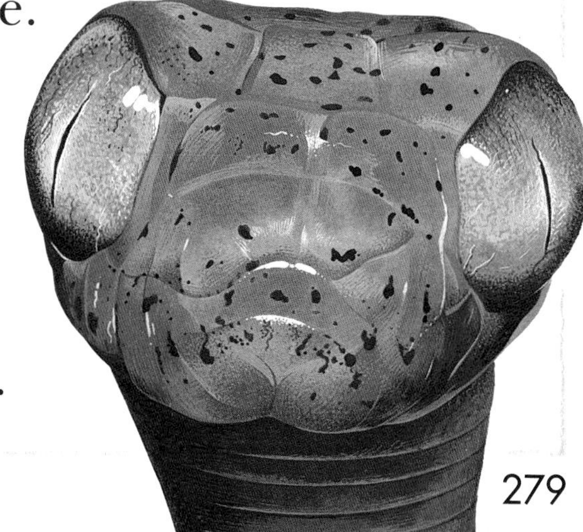

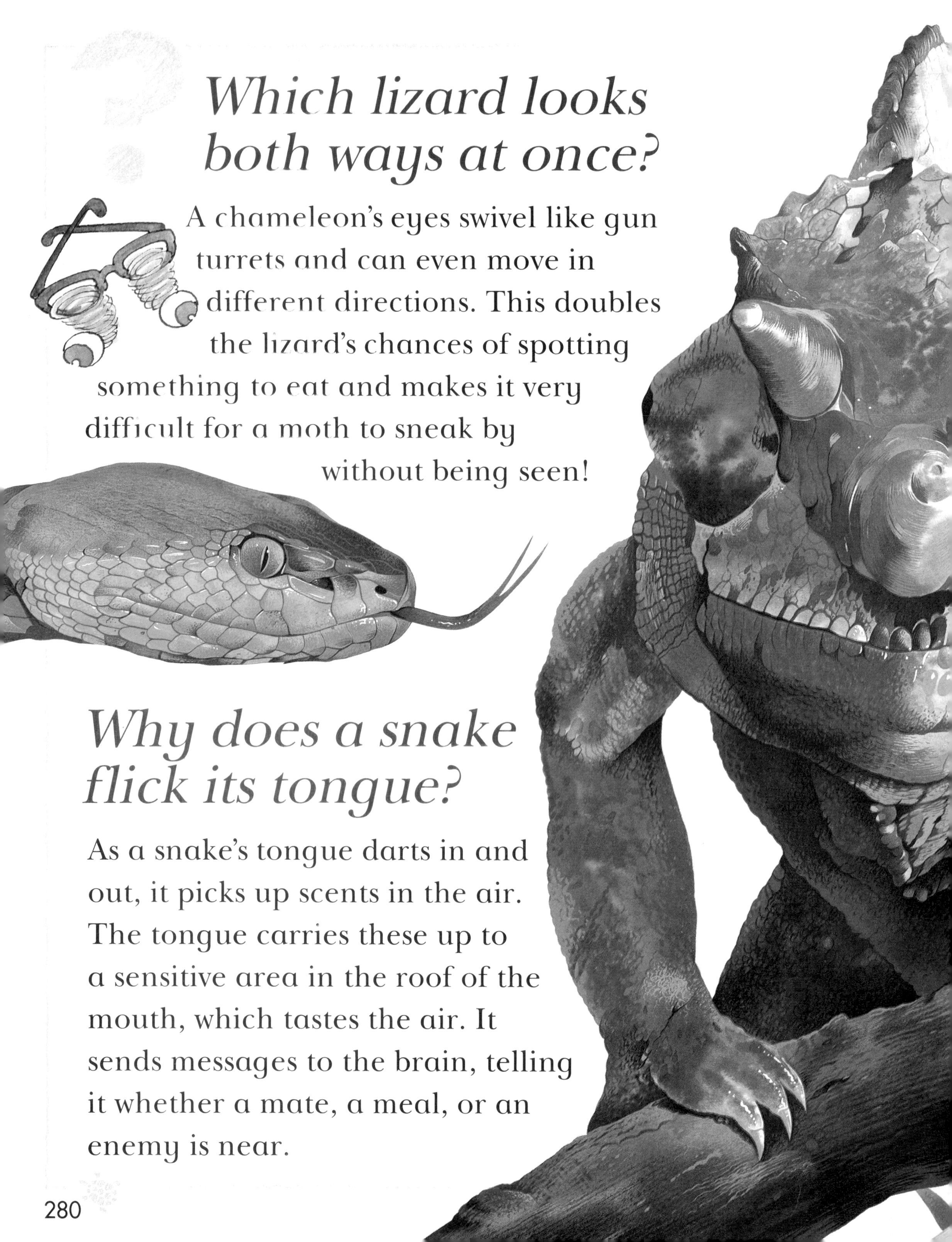

Which lizard looks both ways at once?

A chameleon's eyes swivel like gun turrets and can even move in different directions. This doubles the lizard's chances of spotting something to eat and makes it very difficult for a moth to sneak by without being seen!

Why does a snake flick its tongue?

As a snake's tongue darts in and out, it picks up scents in the air. The tongue carries these up to a sensitive area in the roof of the mouth, which tastes the air. It sends messages to the brain, telling it whether a mate, a meal, or an enemy is near.

• Alligators are the noisiest reptiles. They don't just "talk" to each other, they bellow! In the mating season, males make a great uproar as they try to attract females.

• When the cave anole lizard comes out into the sunshine, it closes its eyes and peeps through scales in its lower eyelids. These protect its eyes like a pair of sunglasses!

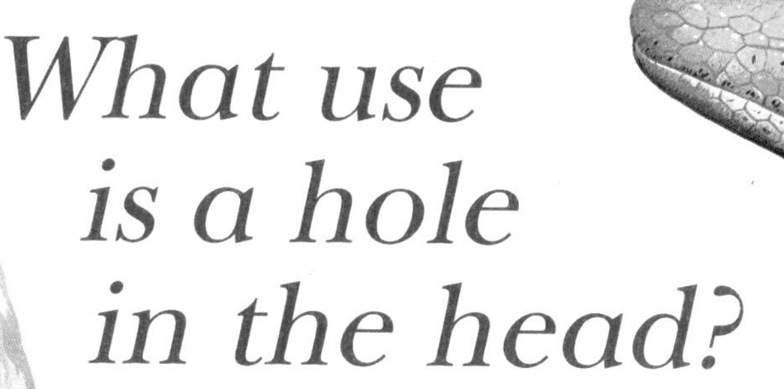

What use is a hole in the head?

If you're a lizard, a hole in the head is very useful—because it's probably an ear! Most lizards have an ear on each side of the head. It's just an open hole leading down to the eardrum inside. Reptiles' ears don't stick out from their heads as ours do. And snakes' ears are hidden inside their heads.

• Rattlesnakes and other pit vipers can hunt in total darkness. They can sense the body heat of a nearby animal and strike their prey with amazing accuracy.

Whose tongue is longer than its tail?

The chameleon's sticky-tipped tongue isn't just longer than its tail, it's longer than its whole body! The lizard shoots it out quick as a wink and reels it back in with a meal.

Why do lizards lose their tails?

Lizards can snap off their tails when they're being attacked. The dropped tail wriggles, puzzling the enemy, and giving the lizard time to escape. A new tail grows in a few weeks.

Why do geckos lick their eyes?

Most lizards have eyelids to wipe their eyes, but the gecko doesn't. Like a snake, it has a scale across the eye. To keep its eyes moist and squeaky clean, the gecko licks them, using its long tongue like a washcloth.

• Most lizards are land-lubbers. The marine iguana from the Galápagos Islands is the only one that swims in the ocean.

Are there still dragons on Earth?

The Komodo dragon may not have wings or breathe fire, but it is truly awesome. It's the world's largest lizard—longer than a car, and heavier than a couple of prizefighters. When people first saw one about 100 years ago, they thought they were looking at a dragon!

Which lizard has a frightful frill?

If you frighten an Australian frilled lizard, it will try to frighten you back. It has a frill of skin around its neck, which it can open up like an umbrella. This makes the lizard look twice its real size. And when it stretches its mouth wide open too, it's a pretty terrifying sight!

- Steer clear of the horned toad from the Southwest. It isn't really a toad, it's a lizard, and it can squirt jets of blood—from its eyes! Scary!

- The African pancake tortoise is well named. It's flat enough to wriggle down a crack in a rock. But then it cleverly puffs itself up, so no enemy can tug it out!

Which turtle kicks up a stink?

The stinkpot turtle has earned its name! When it feels threatened, it lets out a yucky smell that quickly drives away its enemies. And they don't come back!

• The stumpy-tailed skink has a stumpy tail the same shape as its head. As long as it keeps its mouth shut, its enemies can't tell whether the lizard is coming or going!

Why do some snakes pretend to be dead?

Some snakes face danger by pretending that they're dead. The European grass snake rolls on its back and lies quite still with its mouth open and its tongue hanging out. The enemy probably won't want dead snake for lunch and will leave it alone. Then the clever snake comes back to life and makes its escape.

Which reptile is a living fortress?

• Many turtles live in lakes and rivers and others live in the ocean. But some turtles live on land. Turtles that live on land are usually called tortoises.

Living inside a shell is like living inside a fortress. At the first sign of danger, a tortoise retreats inside the shell's thick walls, blocking the "doors" with its feet and claws. It's well protected from attack, and from heat and cold too.

• A tortoise could never park its shell and leave it behind. The shell's horny plates are joined to the skeleton underneath.

Do turtles have teeth?

Turtles don't have teeth, but their horny beaks have plenty of bite. Alligator snapping turtles are particularly fierce. One bite from them and you could lose your toes!

• A tortoise's damaged shell will slowly heal. A vet can help by patching it with fiberglass, a light material used to build boats.

Which turtle breathes through a snorkel?

The spiny soft-shelled turtle spends most of its time under water in rivers and ponds. It doesn't need to come up to the surface to breathe. It pokes its long snout out of the water like a snorkel and draws in a noseful of air.

• Turtles were swimming in the ocean more than 200 million years ago. They're the most ancient of all reptiles.

• A tortoise's shell keeps out most enemies, but eagles and vultures have cracked the problem. They drop the poor animals from a great height and smash their shells.

Do reptiles have skin like ours?

A reptile's skin is quite tough and horny, more like our fingernails than our skin. On snakes and lizards, most of the skin is covered with small scales that overlap one another. But crocodiles and turtles have even tougher skins, with hard plates rather than scales.

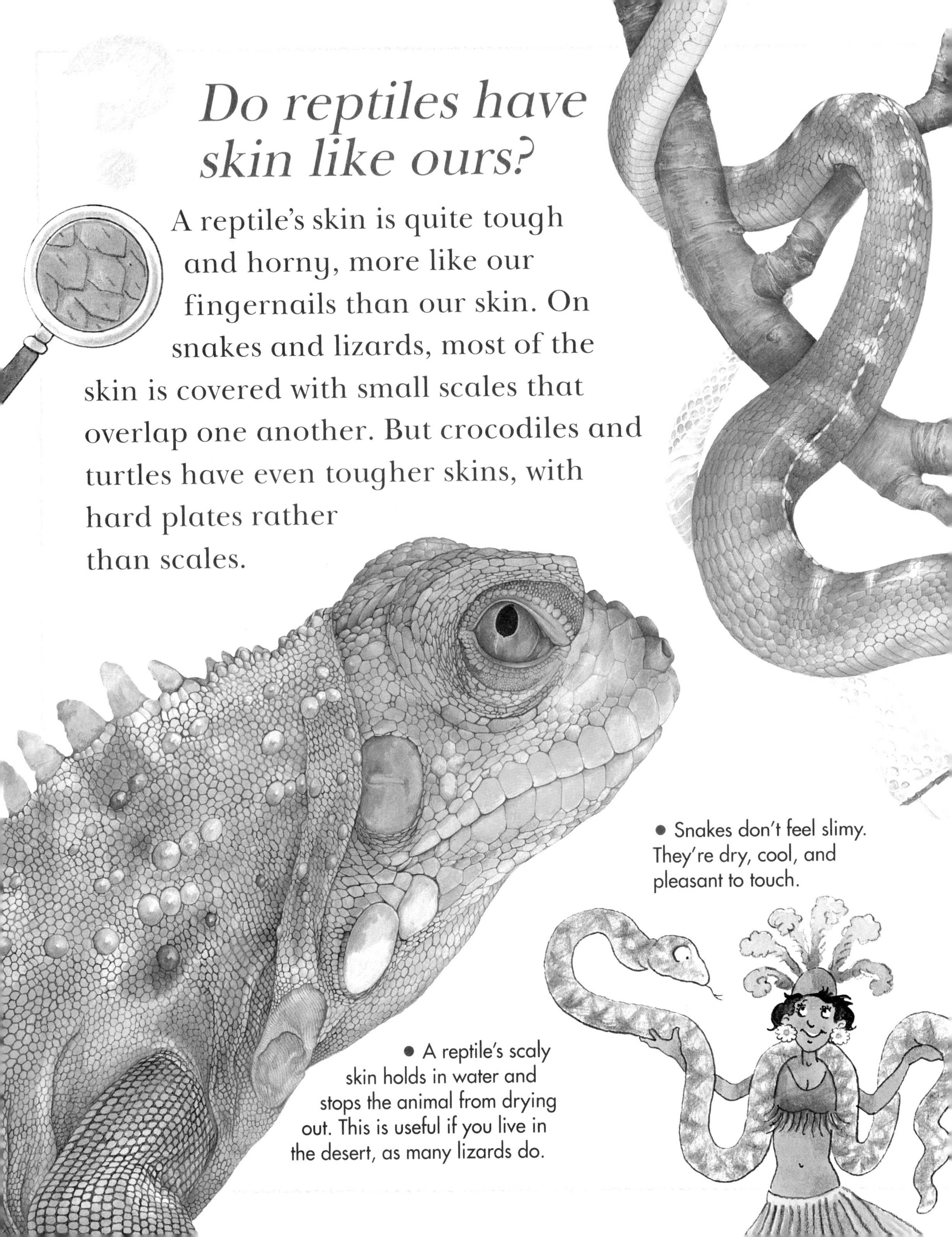

• Snakes don't feel slimy. They're dry, cool, and pleasant to touch.

• A reptile's scaly skin holds in water and stops the animal from drying out. This is useful if you live in the desert, as many lizards do.

• A snake's old skin begins to split at the lips. The snake wriggles out head first, turning the skin inside out as it goes. The skin often comes off in one piece, in a perfect snake shape.

Why do snakes shed their skin?

Like your old clothes, a snake's skin wears out and needs replacing—often in a bigger size. So from three to seven times a year, the old skin splits open and peels off, and—presto!—there's a brand-new skin waiting underneath.

• In times of danger, the armadillo lizard turns into an armored ball. It rolls on its back, grips its tail in its mouth and hides its soft belly behind a wall of scales and spines.

Why do some lizards have horns and spikes?

Horns and spikes are a good way of protecting an animal. Like a strong suit of armor, they make a lizard look fierce —and they also make a prickly mouthful for any animal that tries to attack.

Why do birds have feathers?

Feathers keep birds warm. They also help them to fly, by giving their wings and bodies a special sleek shape.

Each kind of bird has feathers of a different color and pattern. Males are often brighter than females — their good looks help them to attract a mate!

• Birds' fluffy down feathers trap warm air next to their skin just as a comforter keeps you warm in bed.

• Hummingbirds are among the world's smallest birds. The bee hummingbird lays its eggs in a nest the size of a walnut.

Which bird can fly backward?

Hummingbirds are the helicopters of the bird world. They can fly in all directions — backward, forward, sideways, up and down. They can even hover on one spot.

Why can't penguins fly?

• Birds can fly by flapping their wings up and down, or by gliding on still, outstretched wings.

Penguins can't fly because their wings are too small to keep their heavy bodies up in the air. But penguins are very good swimmers and divers. They use their wings as paddles in the water.

• Most birds can fold their wings up close to their bodies, but penguins can't. They always hold their wings stiffly out to the side.

• Ostriches are too big to fly, but they can run at twice the speed of the fastest Olympic runners.

What's inside a bird's egg?

There are three things inside a bird's egg—a baby bird, a yellow yolk, and a clear jelly called the white. The yolk is food for the growing bird. The white is food, too, but it also protects the bird if the egg gets a knock.

• Some eggs don't get the chance to hatch. They are eaten by hungry hunters.

Why do birds turn their eggs?

Birds turn their eggs so that every part of the egg get its fair share of warmth. The baby birds need warmth to grow—that's why a parent has to sit on the nest.

ANIMALS VOLUME II

Which is the biggest creepy-crawly?

The Indonesian giant stick insect is the longest creepy-crawly in the world. At 13 inches long, it would only just fit inside the open pages of this book!

• The heavyweight champion of the creepy-crawly world is the Goliath beetle. It's as heavy as a hamster.

Goliath beetle

• Monarch butterflies hold the world record for long-distance flying. Each year they fly from Canada down to Mexico—a journey of more than 2,000 miles.

• The tropical cockroach is the fastest-known runner in the insect world. It speeds along at more than 3 miles an hour.

Indonesian giant stick insect

Which is the smallest creepy-crawly?

You'd find it hard to see a fairy fly, because it's no bigger than a period. The female lays her tiny eggs inside the eggs of other insects. She can squeeze as many as 20 into just one butterfly egg.

• Before the time of the dinosaurs, monster-sized dragonflies cruised through the air. Some were the size of seagulls!

• The Hercules emperor moth is the world's widest creepy-crawly. From wing to wing, it's the size of a dinner plate!

What is an insect?

An insect has three pairs of legs (that's six altogether), and three parts to its body. The first part is the head, the second is the thorax, and the third is the abdomen.

• Wood lice aren't insects. They belong to the same family as crabs, lobsters, and shrimps. They don't get together very often though, as wood lice live on land, not in water.

• Like all insects, this hoverfly has three pairs of legs and three parts to its body.

Feeler

Head

Eye

Thorax

Mouth

Leg

When is a fly not a fly?

A true fly, such as a housefly, has only one pair of wings. Butterflies, dragonflies, damselflies, and mayflies all have two pairs of wings. So they're not really flies at all!

What is a bug?

Bugs are insects that have needlelike beaks. A bug uses its beak to cut open its food. Then it sucks up the tasty juices inside, using its beak like a straw.

• Bedbugs are the draculas of the insect world. At night, they look for sleeping humans to bite. Then they suck up the tasty blood!

• Centipedes have too many legs to be insects. One kind has 176 pairs!

Are spiders insects?

No—a spider has eight legs, not six. What's more, its body has two parts instead of three. This is because the head and thorax are joined on a spider's body.

• There are more than a million kinds of insect—more than any other kind of animal in the world. And scientists are still finding new ones!

Why do spiders spin webs?

- Most of the webs you see are round orb webs, spun by garden spiders. Other spiders spin webs with different patterns.

A spider's sticky web is its home and its pantry! When an insect flies into the web, it gets stuck. The spider rushes out to spin silk around it. Inside the silk, the insect turns into a liquid mush. Later the spider can suck it up like a drink!

How do spiders make thread?

Spiders make runny silk inside their bodies, drawing it out through little knobs called spinnerets. The runny silk sets into thread, which the spider then weaves into a web, using its spinnerets like fingers.

• A Frenchman once took up spider farming. He soon gave the idea up, but not before he managed to make some spider-silk stockings and gloves.

• All spiders spin silk, but they don't all make webs. The spitting spider catches insects by spitting a sticky gum all over them.

When do spiders fly?

When baby spiders hatch out of their eggs, they spin themselves a long, silk line. Then they wait for the breeze to carry them off through the air to new homes, which may be many hundreds of miles away.

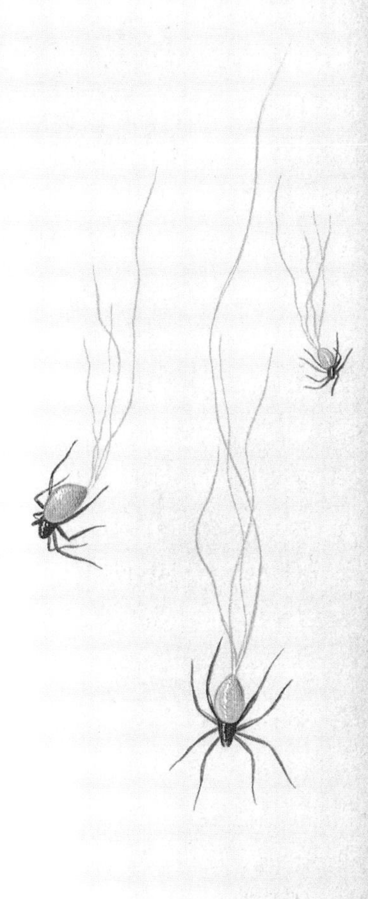

What does an insect feel with its feelers?

Insects use their feelers to taste and smell—the longer the feelers, the better. Some insects also use their feelers like fingers, to check things out by touching.

- A male insect's feelers are often larger than a female's. They help him to scent a female at mating time.

- The male luna moth's feelers are long and feathery. He uses them to locate female moths many miles away by smell.

- The long-horned beetle always fans out its feelers before it flies. They tell it which way the wind is blowing.

- The banded longhorn beetle doesn't just have striped feelers. The rest of it is blue and black, too!

Which insect tastes with its toes?

Most insects taste food with their mouths as we do, but the honeybee can taste with its feet as well. It only needs to land on a flower to sample the dish of the day!

• Spiders have eight eyes, but they're very nearsighted!

Which insect listens with its legs?

The long-horned grasshopper has ears on both its front legs. Its ears don't look like ours, of course. They're tiny holes with skin stretched over the top—a bit like miniature drums.

Why do caterpillars change into butterflies?

Every butterfly has to go through four different stages of its life before it is a fully grown adult. At each stage, it changes its size, its shape, and its color.

• Many kinds of insect change shape as they grow. This way of growing is called metamorphosis.

1 A butterfly lays its eggs on a plant the baby caterpillars eat.

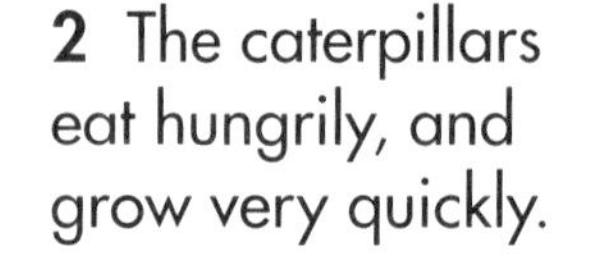

2 The caterpillars eat hungrily, and grow very quickly.

• The babies that hatch from an insect's eggs are known as larvae—but many people just call them grubs.

• Caterpillars grow so quickly that their skin pops open. Underneath, there's brand new skin with plenty of growing room.

3 Each caterpillar makes itself a hard case called a pupa. Inside, its body turns into a kind of mushy soup.

• The pupa is like a strongbox. It keeps the insect's body safe while it changes shape.

• Not all insects change completely as they grow. A grasshopper's eggs hatch out into tiny nymphs, which look almost like their parents.

• Nymphs split their skins as they grow, but they don't make a pupa. They just slowly change into adults.

• A female butterfly lays as many as 50,000 eggs in her lifetime.

4 The soup slowly turns into a butterfly. When the butterfly wriggles out of the pupa, its wings are soft and creased. They dry in the sunlight.

• Butterflies don't need food to grow, but they love to sip sweet nectar from a flower now and then. It's a fuel that helps them to fly.

Which insects wear armor?

Beetles have two pairs of wings, but they only use one pair to fly. The other pair is like a thick piece of armor, covering the beetle's delicate wings and soft body.

1 When a beetle is scuttling along the ground, its flying wings are hidden beneath a shiny armored wing casing.

2 When it wants to fly, a beetle opens its armor casing and stretches out its wings.

△ It's not difficult to guess how the giraffe weevil got its name. Its neck is twice as long as its body!

Which beetle fires a spray gun?

Watch out for the bombardier beetle! It shoots its enemies with a jet of hot, stinging liquid. As the jet is fired, it makes a sharp cracking sound like a tiny gun going off.

What digs graves, then robs them?

Burying beetles have no respect for the dead! When they find a dead animal, they dig away the soil until the body sinks into the ground. Then they lay their eggs inside the body and cover it with soil. When the eggs hatch out, there's a tasty, well-stocked meat store waiting for them!

• Imagine rolling balls of snow to make a snowman. That's how scarab beetles roll their balls of animal dung. They push the balls into a safe hiding place, and eat them later on.

• Ancient Egyptians thought the Sun was rolled across the sky by a giant scarab beetle.

3 The beetle beats its wings and moves smoothly through the air.

Which insect makes the best mother?

A mother earwig spends all winter looking after her eggs. She licks them clean and keeps them warm. When they hatch, she feeds them with food brought up from her stomach. Yummy!

• A wood louse carries her babies in a pouch, just as kangaroos do!

What hatches out in a vase?

The potter wasp makes tiny vases from wet clay. She lays an egg in each one and pushes in a live caterpillar, sealing the vase so that the caterpillar can't escape. When the baby wasp hatches out, its first meal is waiting for it!

Which insect is the laziest parent?

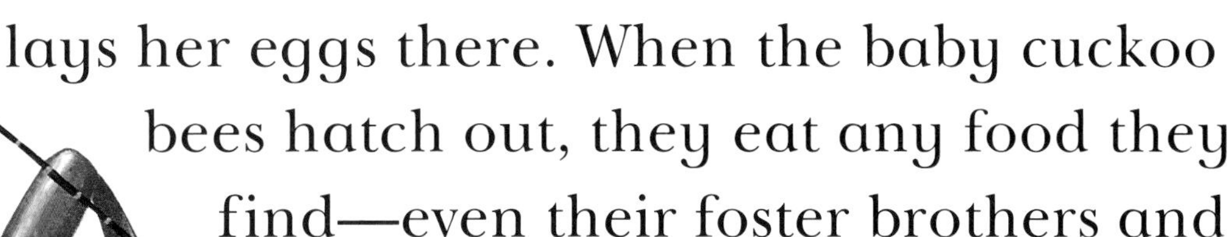

The cuckoo bee doesn't look after her own babies. Instead, she sneaks into another bee's nest and lays her eggs there. When the baby cuckoo bees hatch out, they eat any food they find—even their foster brothers and sisters!

• A queen bee lays up to 3,500 eggs a day, for several weeks at a time. No wonder she only lives for a couple of years!

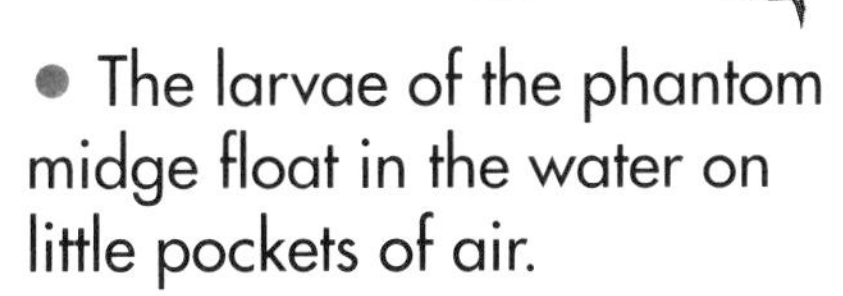

• The larvae of the phantom midge float in the water on little pockets of air.

• The wolf spider carries her eggs around in a silk backpack. When the babies hatch out, they climb out onto her back and ride piggyback.

When is a flower not a flower?

When it's a flower mantis! This insect is not only as pink as a flower, its body has knobbly parts that are shaped like petals. When an insect lands on the "flower" to feed, the mantis grabs it and eats it up.

• The treehopper is a tiny bug with a sharp disguise. When it sits on a twig, the shape of its back makes it look just like a thorn.

• If a bird swoops on a peacock butterfly, it gets a nasty shock! When the butterfly's wings open, they look just like a fierce pair of eyes.

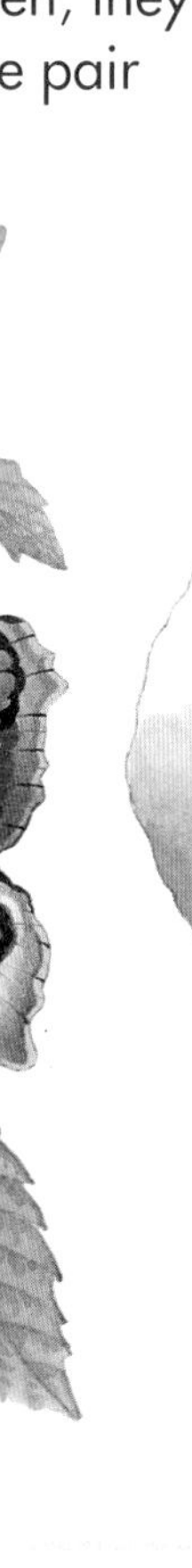

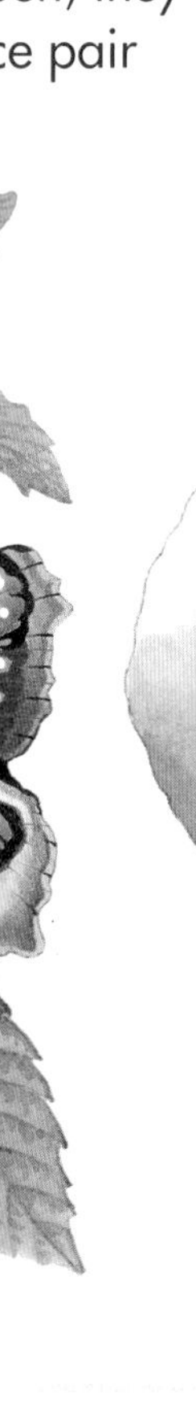

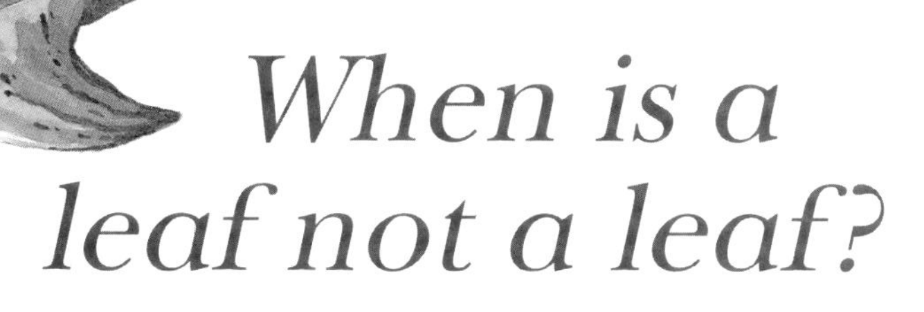

When is a leaf not a leaf?

Leaf insects disguise themselves as leaves to hide from their enemies. Their green, leaf-shaped bodies are even crisscrossed with lines that look like the veins on a real leaf.

◁ This bee's black and yellow stripes mean, "Danger! I sting!" Hoverflies don't sting—but they wear a bee's coat to pretend that they do.

Which insect has a fierce bottom?

The Australian hawkmoth's caterpillar scares off its enemies by waving its bottom at them! The back end of its body looks like a fierce face with two bright circles for eyes. An attacking bird soon flies off in a hurry!

Why do bees live in hives?

In the wild, families of honeybees live in holes in a tree or a rock. But if a friendly beekeeper provides a couple of cozy hives, then the bees are very happy to move in. This is really to help the beekeeper, of course—collecting honey from a hive is much easier than climbing a tree!

• When beekeepers open a hive, they wear special coveralls, gloves, and veils to protect themselves from beestings.

Why do bees dance?

When a honeybee finds plenty of food, it flies back to the hive to tell its friends. It does this by dancing. The number of wiggles in the dance and the direction the bee points tell the other bees exactly where to go.

• Bees not only have a brush, they have a comb! It's on their front legs, and they use it to clean their feelers.

• Collecting nectar to make honey is hard work. A bee would have to make 10 million trips to get enough for a single jar!

Why do bees carry brushes and baskets?

Honeybees have little baskets on their back legs and brushes of hair on their other legs. When a bee lands on a flower, it brushes a powder called pollen into its baskets. Then it flies back to the hive to feed the pollen to its young.

• Bears rob honey from bees' nests. Their thick fur protects them from bee stings —except on the nose!

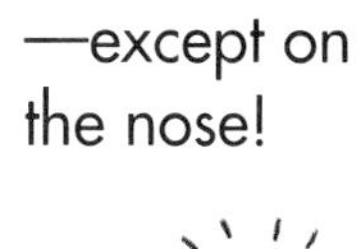

• Not all bees like to live in hives. Many kinds of bee live alone, in burrows.

Which ants live in a tent?

Weaver ants sew leaves together to make tents for themselves, and they use their larvae as needles and thread! Each ant holds a young grub in its mouth, and pokes it through the edges of two leaves. The grub makes a sticky, silky thread, which stitches the two leaves firmly together.

Whose house has a trap door?

The trap-door spider's burrow has a door with a silk hinge which can open and shut. The spider hides inside, waiting for passing insects. When it hears one, it flings up the trap door and grabs its victim.

• Many creepy-crawlies make their homes in your home. Ants, spiders, moths, centipedes, and houseflies all like to live indoors.

Whose nest is paper thin?

The paper wasp's nest has paper walls. It makes the paper by chewing up strips of wood, which it tears from plants or old fence posts! It spreads the mixture in thin layers to build the nest.

• A tent caterpillar spins a shady silk canopy, and shelters under it while it feeds.

• Termites are champion builders, and make mud nests up to four times taller than a man. They need the room—as many as 5 million termites may be living inside!

What has a sting in its tail?

A scorpion attacks by curving its tail over its head. It stabs its prey with the sharp end of its tail, and then squirts out poison. Ouch!

Can spiders kill people?

Although spider bites can hurt a lot, very few are poisonous enough to kill you. The black widow is the best-known deadly spider. Her poison is powerful enough to kill a human. She has another nasty habit, too—sometimes she eats her mate!

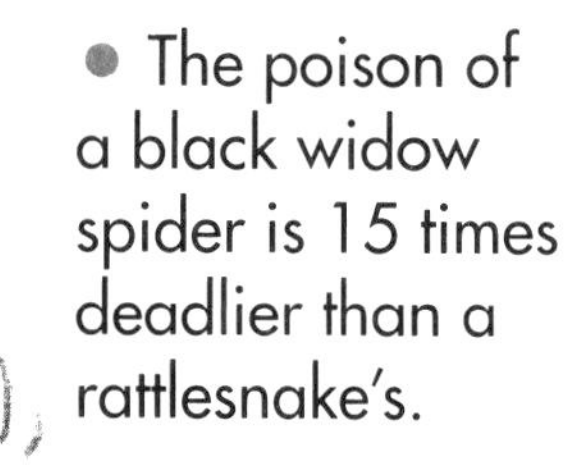

• The poison of a black widow spider is 15 times deadlier than a rattlesnake's.

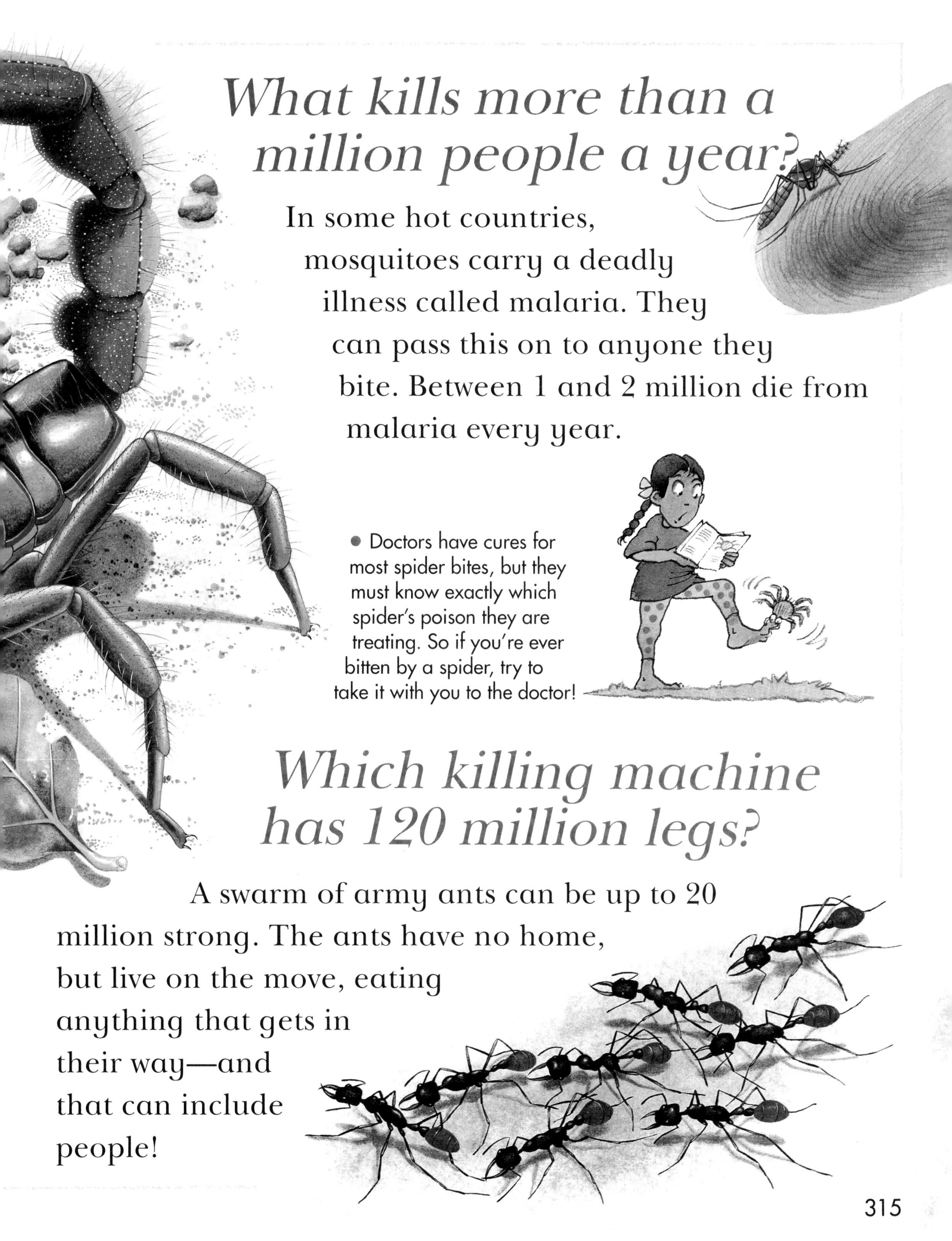

What kills more than a million people a year?

In some hot countries, mosquitoes carry a deadly illness called malaria. They can pass this on to anyone they bite. Between 1 and 2 million die from malaria every year.

• Doctors have cures for most spider bites, but they must know exactly which spider's poison they are treating. So if you're ever bitten by a spider, try to take it with you to the doctor!

Which killing machine has 120 million legs?

A swarm of army ants can be up to 20 million strong. The ants have no home, but live on the move, eating anything that gets in their way—and that can include people!

Are creepy-crawlies good for people?

Most creepy-crawlies are harmless—and some of them are valuable friends. They help plants to grow, keep the earth clean, and give us things such as silk to wear and honey to eat.

• People who study insects are called entomologists. They travel all around the world, learning about insects and trying to protect them.

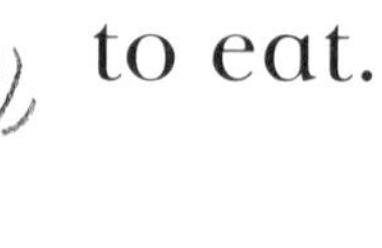

• How would you feel about eating a toasted grasshopper? In different parts of the world, grasshoppers and caterpillars are served as tasty tidbits.

• Insects are the world's garbage collectors, eating up mucky things like dung and dead bodies.

• True locusts aren't good for people. They do more damage, more quickly, than any other insect. Locusts can gather in their millions and strip a crop field in minutes.

• Ladybugs are a gardener's best friend. They protect garden plants by eating huge numbers of hungry caterpillars and aphids.

• Rain forests are home to more insects than anywhere else in the world.

Are people good for creepy-crawlies?

Many creepy-crawlies gain by having us around. Our homes give them food, warmth, and shelter. But others have suffered because we've destroyed their homes or their food.

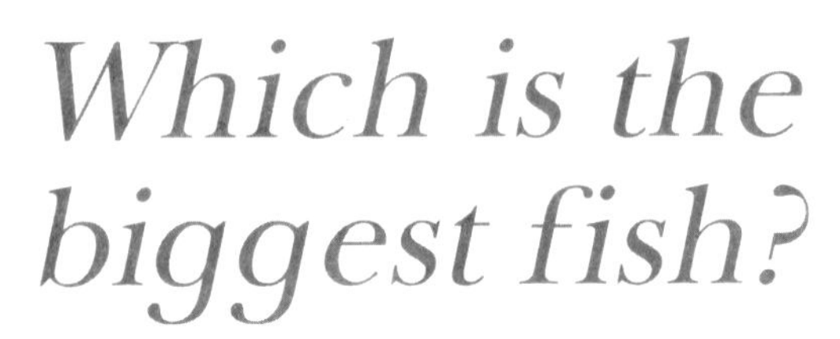

Which is the biggest fish?

The whale shark is the world's biggest fish. It's gigantic—as long as eight scuba divers lying head to toe, and as heavy as six large elephants.

• The dwarf goby is the smallest fish in the ocean.

• The oarfish is the longest fish in the ocean—as long as four canoes placed end to end.

Oarfish

• The biggest sea plant is the giant kelp seaweed. A single strand can grow nearly as long as a football field!

Sailfish

Which is the fastest fish?

The sailfish can race along under water more than 60 miles an hour—as fast as a car. It tucks its fins in tightly, and its pointed nose cuts through the water like a knife.

Whale shark

Which is the biggest crab?

• The pea-sized pea crab is the smallest crab of all. It lives inside oyster and mussel shells.

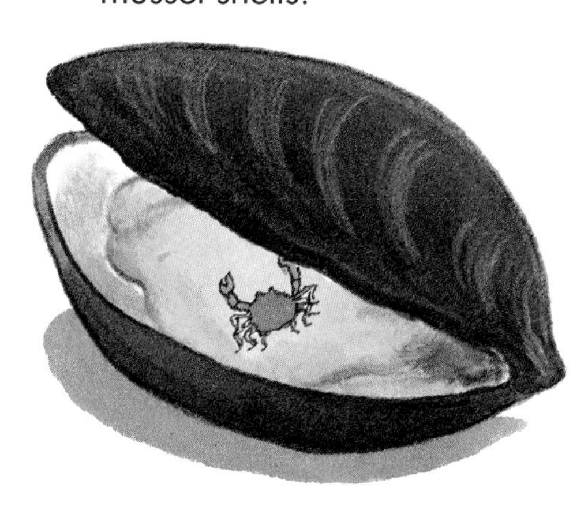

Japan's giant spider crab measures nearly 13 feet from the tip of one front claw to the tip of the other. It could open its arms wide enough to hug a hippopotamus!

How do fish breathe under water?

▷ Not all sea creatures can breathe under water. Sea cows, seals, and dolphins breathe air, so they have to keep coming to the surface.

Fish have to breathe to stay alive, just as you do. But while you breathe oxygen from the air, fish take it from water. As they swim, fish gulp in water and push it out through slits called gills on their heads. Oxygen passes from the water into the fish's blood inside their gills.

Gill cover

How do fish swim?

Fish swim by using their muscles to ripple their bodies along. Wiggling their tails from side to side gives them extra push. They use their other fins to balance and change direction.

Which bird flies under water?

Penguins can't fly through the air because their wings are too short and stumpy. They are much more at home in the ocean, where they use their wings as flippers.

Which animal is jet-propelled?

• Seahorses aren't strong swimmers. They hang on to seaweed to avoid being swept away.

Squid don't have flippers or a tail, but they're still fast movers. They suck water into their bodies, then squirt it out so powerfully that their bodies shoot backward.

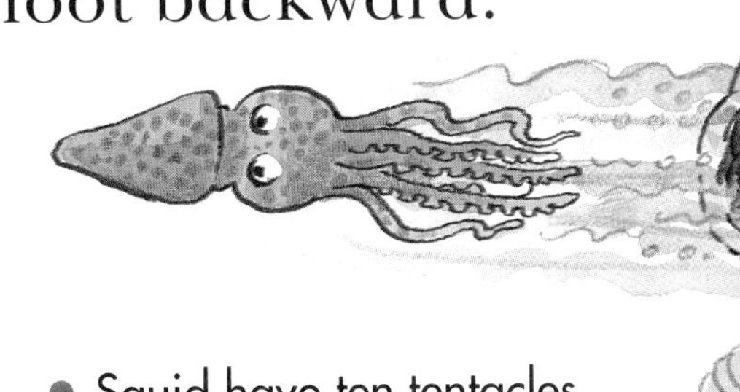

• Squid have ten tentacles—that's two more than their relative, the octopus.

Which fish has headlights?

• The deep sea is inky black and as cold as a refrigerator. Even so, some amazing creatures live there.

Some fish make their own light at the bottom of the dark ocean. The anglerfish has a long fleshy "rod" dangling in front of its face. At the end of the rod is a blob that glows. Small fish are drawn toward the glowing light, only to disappear into the angler-fish's big, gaping mouth.

Anglerfish

How deep is the ocean?

• The seabed has huge cracks in it, called trenches. Some are more than 6 miles deep.

Away from the shore, the ocean plunges to more than 2 miles in most places. That's deep enough to swallow 10 Empire State Buildings, one on top of the other!

What makes chimneys under the sea?

Fountains of boiling hot water gush out of holes in some parts of the seabed. Tiny grains sink down out of the hot water and build into weird-looking chimney stacks around the holes.

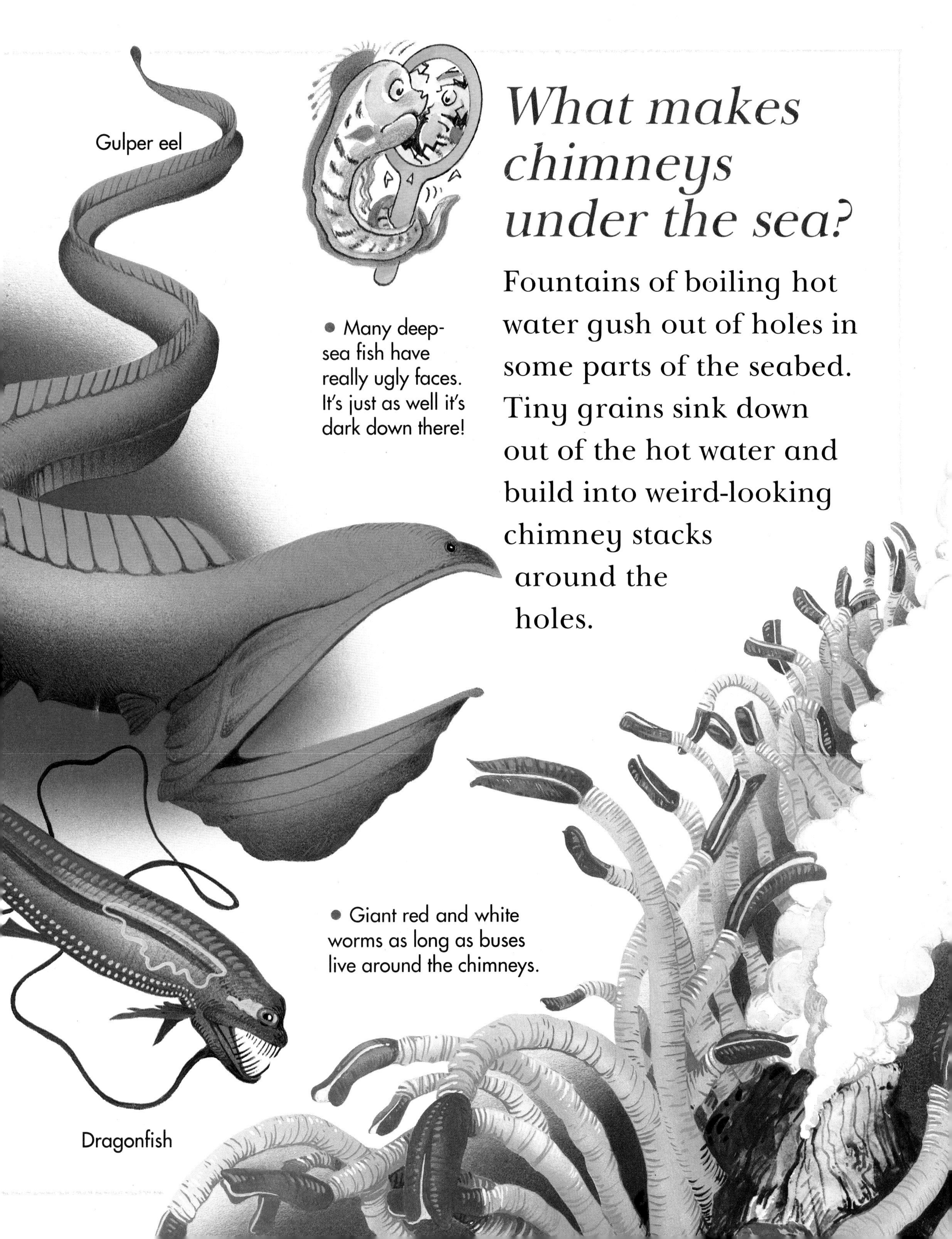

• Many deep-sea fish have really ugly faces. It's just as well it's dark down there!

• Giant red and white worms as long as buses live around the chimneys.

Where do angels, clowns, and parrots live?

Angelfish, clown fish, and parrot fish are just some of the thousands of beautiful animals that live on coral reefs. Tropical fish like these often have dazzling colors and bold patterns.

• Coral reefs grow in shallow water in the warmest parts of the world.

• Giant clams live on coral reefs. Their shells are big enough to take a bath in!

What is a coral reef?

• Corals come in all sorts of shapes—antlers, plates, mushrooms, feathers, daisies, and even brains!

A coral reef is like a beautiful underwater hedge. It looks stony and dead—but it is really alive! Coral is made up of millions of tiny animals that leave their hard skeletons behind when they die. Each new layer piles on to the old, slowly building the coral rock.

Where is the biggest reef?

The world's biggest coral reef lies in warm shallow seas off the northeast coast of Australia. It's called the Great Barrier Reef, and it stretches for more than 1,200 miles. It's so huge that it can be seen by astronauts up in space.

Clown fish

Which fish hunts with a hammer?

The hammerhead shark has a huge head shaped like a hammer. But this tool is for hunting, not banging in nails. The shark's eyes and nostrils are at each end of the hammer. As the shark swims, it swings its head from side to side, searching for a meal.

Which is the most shocking fish?

Some fish give off electric shocks to protect themselves or to stun animals they want to eat. The most shocking ocean fish is the torpedo ray. If you could switch it on, it would light up a light bulb!

• The Portuguese man-of-war catches its meal in its long, stinging tentacles.

• Thousands of mackerel swim together in one huge school. Their enemies find it difficult to pick out a single fish from the shimmering, silvery mass.

Which fish look like stones?

Stonefish look just like lumps of stone, or rock—but they're far more dangerous. If attacked, a stonefish uses the needle-sharp spines on its fins to stab its enemy with a deadly poison.

• The leafy sea dragon looks just like a ragged strand of seaweed. What a perfect disguise!

Which animals shoot their food?

If an archer fish spots an insect sitting on a plant above the water, it shoots it — not with an arrow or a bullet, of course, but with a jet of water squirted from its mouth. The insect falls into the water and the fish gobbles it up.

• The bolas spider swings a thread with a sticky blob at the end to catch insects. A bolas is a kind of lasso used by South American cowboys.

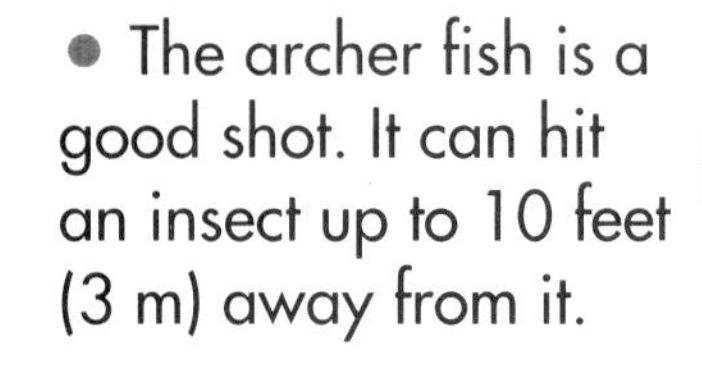

• The archer fish is a good shot. It can hit an insect up to 10 feet (3 m) away from it.

• The sound of the pistol shrimp's big left pincer snapping shut sends shock waves through the water, stunning small fish and making them easier to catch.

Index

This index will help you to find out where you can read information about a subject. It is in alphabetical order. Each section is under a large letter of the alphabet. A main entry and its page numbers are printed in **dark**, or **bold**, letters. This is where you will find the most information. Other page numbers show where you can find further information.

Acknowledgements

The publishers would like to thank the following
artists for their contribution to this book:

Susanna Addario 166–167, 208–209; **Simone Boni** (Virgil Pomfret Agency) 222–223; **Peter Cornwell** 212; **Joanne Cowne** 274–275; **Peter Dennis** (Linda Rogers Associates) 126–127, 154–157, 214–215, 234–235, 238–245; **Micheal Fisher** 124–125, 130–131; **Chris Forsey** 14–15, 32–52, 55*br*, 58–59, 62*tl*, 63*tr*, 65*tr*, 67*tr*, 68–73, 76–83, 86–89, 92*tl*, 94–97, 104–107, 112–115, 120–123, 128–129, 132, 162–163, 164*tr*, 168–170, 174–179, 186–187, 196–197, 216–217, 224–227, 230–231, 248–249, 252, 267, 276–277, 282–283, 294–295, 316–319; **Terry Gabbey** (AFA Ltd) 136–139, 160–161, 198–199, 246–247; **Luigi Galante** (Virgil Pomfret Agency) 180–181, 192–193, 250–251; **Ruby Green** 54–55, 62–63, 66–67, 71*br*, 74–75, 92, 150–151, 158–159; **Craig Greenwood** (Wildlife Art Agency) 220–221; **Nick Harris** (Virgil Pomfret Agency) 142–143; **Stephen Holmes** 254–261, 268–273, 290–291, 308–309, 312–313, 328; **Adam Hook** (Linden Artists) 200*tl*; 204*tl*, **Christa Hook** (Linden Artists) 200–201; **Christian Hook** 140–141, 194–195, 210–211, 264–265; **Biz Hull** (Artist Partners) 56–57, 60–61, 64–65, 134–135, 146–147, 164–165, 262–263; **Tony Kenyon** (BL Kearley) all cartoons; **Adrian Lascom** (Garden Studio) 296–297, 300–301; **Alan Male** (Linden Artists) 286–287, 304–307, 314–315; **Angus McBride** (Linden Artists) 228–229; **David Mitcheson** 204–205; **Nicki Palin** 144–145, 148–149, 152–153, 182–185, 202, 206–207, 218–219, 232–233, 236–237, 288–289, 310–311, 314*tl*; **Maurice Pledger** (Bernard Thornton Artists) 320–321; **Bryan Poole** 322–327; **Sebastian Quigley** (Linden Artists) 16–23, 26–27, 98–99; **Claudia Saraceni** 190–191; **Stephen Seymour** (Bernard Thornton Artists) 110–111*m*; **Roger Stewart** (Virgil Pomfret Agency) 118–119; **Ian Thompson** 24–25, 28–31, 100–101; **Richard Ward** 116–117, 188–189; **Russ Watton** (Garden Studio) 102–103, 108–109, 110*b*, 111*r*, 202*tl*, 203*ml*; **Linda Worrall** (Linden Artists) 84–85, 86*ml*, 90–91; **David Wright** (Kathy Jakeman) 278–281, 284–285, 292, 298–299, 302–303.